Mastering Microsoft Teams

End User Guide to Practical Usage, Collaboration, and Governance

Second Edition

Melissa Hubbard
Matthew J. Bailey
D'arce Hess
Mårten Hellebro

Apress®

Mastering Microsoft Teams: End User Guide to Practical Usage, Collaboration, and Governance

Melissa Hubbard
Dumfries, VA, USA

Matthew J. Bailey
Falls Church, VA, USA

D'arce Hess
East Greenwich, RI, USA

Mårten Hellebro
New York, NY, USA

ISBN-13 (pbk): 978-1-4842-6897-1
https://doi.org/10.1007/978-1-4842-6898-8

ISBN-13 (electronic): 978-1-4842-6898-8

Managing Director, Apress Media LLC: Welmoed Spahr
Acquisitions Editor: Joan Murray
Development Editor: Laura Berendson
Coordinating Editor: Jill Balzano

Cover image designed by Freepik (www.freepik.com)

Distributed to the book trade worldwide by Springer Science+Business Media LLC, 1 New York Plaza, Suite 4600, New York, NY 10004. Phone 1-800-SPRINGER, fax (201) 348-4505, e-mail orders-ny@springer-sbm.com, or visit www.springeronline.com. Apress Media, LLC is a California LLC and the sole member (owner) is Springer Science + Business Media Finance Inc (SSBM Finance Inc). SSBM Finance Inc is a **Delaware** corporation.

For information on translations, please e-mail booktranslations@springernature.com; for reprint, paperback, or audio rights, please e-mail bookpermissions@springernature.com.

Apress titles may be purchased in bulk for academic, corporate, or promotional use. eBook versions and licenses are also available for most titles. For more information, reference our Print and eBook Bulk Sales web page at http://www.apress.com/bulk-sales.

Any source code or other supplementary material referenced by the author in this book is available to readers on GitHub via the book's product page, located at www.apress.com/9781484268971. For more detailed information, please visit http://www.apress.com/source-code.

Printed on acid-free paper

D'arce's Dedication

This book is dedicated to my parents Deena and Jim who have always encouraged me to take the road less traveled.

Mårten's Dedication

To the love of my life, my best friend, and my lifesaver, Ann-Louise. Thank you for always believing in me and making me understand what's most important in life. You bring out the best in me, and us, and our fantastic children. Amanda, Jacob, and Matilda, Daddy will be with you shortly, just one second... Love you forever.

Table of Contents

About the Authors

Melissa Hubbard specializes in driving productivity, collaboration, and communication in the modern workplace. She is a former Microsoft MVP and early adopter of Microsoft Teams, with a background in project management and implementation of collaboration and business process automation solutions. User adoption, governance, and training are topics she is especially passionate about.

Matthew J. Bailey is a Microsoft MVP and Microsoft Certified Trainer (MCT) for Noteworthy Technology Training, specializing in SharePoint, Office 365 (including Teams), Azure, and Power BI. He combines his business expertise and his technical knowledge to resolve corporate challenges. He is a highly regarded presenter, avid blogger, and author, most recently of *The SharePoint Business Analyst Guide*.

D'arce Hess is a Microsoft MVP who specializes in the creation of custom portals and experiences in SharePoint, Microsoft Teams, and Office 365. As a UI/UX designer and developer, she uses industry and Microsoft best practices as a base for creating solutions that simplify processes and drive user adoption and governance from the start. She has worked with Fortune 500 companies and has become a trusted partner to her clients in the industries of healthcare, pharmaceuticals, legal, travel and tourism, and entertainment. She loves to volunteer in the community and is the leader of the Rhode Island SharePoint & Office 365 User Group.

Mårten Hellebro is an Office Apps and Services MVP focused on Microsoft Teams and an expert in enterprise voice. As an infrastructure, migration, and user adoption lead, Mårten has extensive experience from managing numerous Teams and Skype for Business implementation projects. He regularly speaks at Microsoft conferences and other events, and he is the head organizer of the largest Microsoft Teams conference in the Nordics "Teamsdagen." He also runs the Microsoft Teams blog msteamsswe.se and is one of two hosts of the Microsoft Teams podcast "Teamspodden" and co-organizes the Swedish Unified Communication User Group. He is pleased to guide customers on their journey from Skype for Business to Microsoft Teams.

About the Technical Reviewer

Albert-Jan Schot, also known as Appie, is someone who lives and breathes Microsoft 365 to such a degree that it has become second nature to him. He has numerous certifications to his name. With his extensive knowledge, Albert-Jan is a valuable source of information for colleagues. Albert-Jan not only enjoys stepping up to the challenge of designing, developing, and building innovative cloud solutions, he also has consultancy and training experience. He is active on a range of forums, blogs, as well as on Twitter where he shares his knowledge and passion with others. Over the years, he had the opportunity to present at several national and international user groups and events.

Introduction

Microsoft Teams is the heart of collaboration and communications within Office 365. As Microsoft Teams has matured over time, it has brought deep integrations with your favorite Office applications and offered ways to integrate with your internal business processes. In order for organizations to fully appreciate Microsoft Teams, end users must have an understanding of how to use its features. To truly appreciate Microsoft Teams and drive user adoption from the start, business owners and administrators should have a firm understanding of how to provide governance and training. With work landscapes changing from being in an office to including more remote working scenarios, the opportunities to connect colleagues, students and teachers, and customers have never been more vital. In this book, all of these scenarios are addressed and more.

Mastering Microsoft Teams is for anyone that has never used Microsoft Teams as well as anyone that has already been using Microsoft Teams in a work or school environment, but wants to learn more. Additionally, business owners and IT professionals will benefit from learning additional ways to support end users through governance and extendability.

The layout of this book begins by answering what Microsoft Teams is, followed by chapters on how to work, communicate, hold meetings, and extend capabilities. These chapters provide step-by-step guidance on how to perform different actions, as well as tips and tricks to help you get the most out of the application. Additional chapters focus on improving user adoption and the creation and implementation of a governance plan to provide a safe and secure way to allow collaboration within your organization. The remaining chapter focuses on using Microsoft Teams in the classroom by providing instructions for both educators and students to help navigate a world of remote learning opportunities.

Microsoft Teams is continuously updated with additional functionality. Depending on when you are reading this book, we acknowledge that many things have changed already. This being said, we have included a chapter discussing known issues with the limitations of Microsoft Teams and look at some of the updates that are planned for the future.

CHAPTER 1

Introduction to Microsoft Teams

If you are reading this book, it is highly likely that you have heard some of the excitement surrounding Microsoft Teams. Understanding the value of the application and knowing about its components and how they interact with each other is a good way to start learning about the product. In this chapter, we explain the different methods of accessing Microsoft Teams and the different features that combine to make it work. If you're ready to begin your journey of learning Microsoft Teams, without further ado, let's begin!

In today's working world, we all struggle with being on a short schedule, trying to connect with remote workers, and getting our job tasks completed on time. Often there are many people required to work on the same information or documents to accomplish a task. People's work is spread across multiple locations, making it time-consuming and confusing to multitask. These business problems can be resolved with Microsoft Teams.

Chat, meetings, video and voice calls, document collaboration, file storage and sharing, retrieving information, notes, third-party tool integration, and more have been combined into a hub for teamwork into the Microsoft Teams platform. Microsoft Teams can be thought of as one "super application" that integrates many different apps into one program so that you don't have to open and connect to many apps separately.

Our favorite description of the product is this: "If someone put Skype for Business/ Skype, Outlook's meetings and mailbox, Office 365 Groups, a persistent chat client, Word/Excel/PowerPoint, OneDrive for Business, a SharePoint site collection, Firstline worker scheduling software, and Azure Active Directory (AAD), then mixed them together and cooked them in the oven, Microsoft Teams would pop out." You can then "season to taste" by adding countless different other apps from Office 365 or outside companies to make a recipe of your own.

© Melissa Hubbard, Matthew J. Bailey, D'arce Hess, Mårten Hellebro 2021
M. Hubbard et al., *Mastering Microsoft Teams*, https://doi.org/10.1007/978-1-4842-6898-8_1

Examples of other Microsoft apps you can add to a team are Microsoft Planner for project management, Visual Studio Team Services for developer teams, a specific SharePoint site for storage or collaboration, Power BI for data visualization, PowerApps for semicomplex form creation, Stream for video, or Forms for simple data collection. Some examples of non-Microsoft apps that you could add include GitHub for developer's code, Jira for project management, Adobe Sign for electronic signature collection, and Hootsuite for social media monitoring.

Although Chapter 5 goes into more about real-world use cases for Microsoft Teams, Figures 1-1 and 1-2 show how to set up and use a team. First, let's start with what a new, blank team looks like.

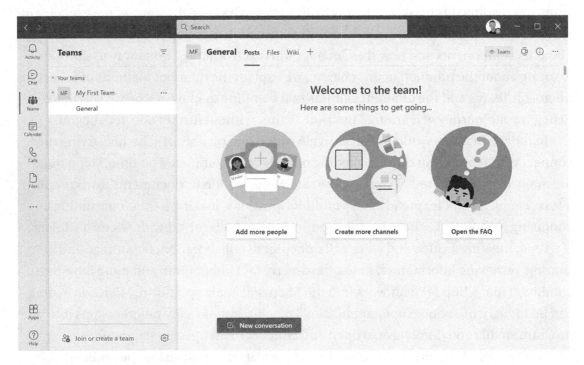

Figure 1-1. *A brand-new empty team*

As you can see in Figure 1-1, there is not too much happening in a new team. Think of it as an empty "virtual office" waiting to be filled with other co-workers or associates, discussions, files, projects, and video calls. Microsoft Teams is a part of Microsoft's *modern workplace*, a vision that allows distributed people to work together in a digital, flexible workspace.

As an example of what a team can look like in production, Figure 1-2 is a quick screenshot of a team used for a new product launch. The team has added channels, tabs, applications such as Adobe Sign and Power BI, files, meetings, chats, and many of the other things that a team uses while working on a project. But don't be overwhelmed! There is a lot to learn as you make your journey through this book. Showing you what is possible helps you get excited in learning it! Figure 1-2 shows what an active team with lots of activity looks like.

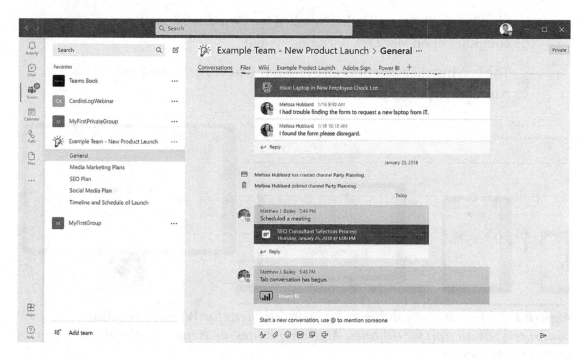

Figure 1-2. *An example team for a new product launch with lots of activity and interaction*

Microsoft Teams is very fluid and can be used for many different purposes. A team working on a new product launch, a group of people working to develop and launch a small software product, or even authors collaborating to write a book are just a few examples of why people might use Microsoft Teams.

Having a goal of how you like to work, what you want to work on, and who you want to work with should be a part of every team's setup process. We review these topics in more depth in upcoming chapters.

How to Use and Access Teams

As you see in Figure 1-3, Teams is accessible via three different methods. Each format that you access a team in places slightly different parameters around what you can do with it. As an example, you currently have the option to access a team through the following ways:

- Your Internet browser by accessing your Office 365 tenant

- The Teams client application installed on a Windows-based computer or on Mac OSX operating system

- The app installed on either an iOS-based (Apple) or an Android-based smartphone

Figure 1-3. *Teams is available as an installed client for Windows or Mac computers; as an app for iPhones, Android phones, or Windows phones; and via some web browsers*

What you will probably notice first is that based on which type of client you are accessing, you have different features available to you. In the case of the Internet site or Windows client vs. the smartphone app, this is pretty much an industry standard. Most phone apps are not quite able to provide as much functionality as the other ways an application might be created. For the most part, enough features exist on all platforms to use the product successfully. Just be aware that the product has variances, and because it is new to the market, it will continue to have many features being added, changed, or updated on its different clients.

Background: The Journey from Skype

Teams was built by the Skype for Business product group at Microsoft. Skype for Business will eventually become Microsoft Teams; however, it is important to note that this is a longer-term vision and not something that will happen immediately. At the moment, there is still a Skype for Business 2019 version planned to roll out that will be supported for many years. At the moment, Microsoft Teams is *only* available in the cloud; it is not available to be installed on local servers. Although Teams works with an on-premises installation of Microsoft Exchange (one of the pieces of Teams), it is important to note that currently some of the features, such as eDiscovery for Teams, will not work in that scenario.

As a quick point of reference, to utilize all the functionality that Teams has available and the new features continually being added, you need to be fully in the cloud on the Office 365 suite and all the related applications (SharePoint, Exchange, Skype for Business, and OneDrive for Business).

It is also important to note that although Microsoft Teams is built in part from Skype for Business, not all the features from Skype for Business are available in Teams at the moment. According to the Microsoft road map, however, they are in progress and should be delivered in the near future (or have already been delivered, depending upon when you are reading this book).

What Is Included When Creating a Team

Microsoft Teams is a combination of different applications rolled into one. However, there are some key ingredients that allow Teams to function. Each time you create a new team, the following items are created in the background on Microsoft's servers outside of Teams:

- Office 365 Groups (Modern Groups) – unless you choose an existing group when you add a team

- SharePoint site collection (with a document library)

- Exchange Online group mailbox

When you are using Microsoft Teams, it might not be immediately apparent that you are using these other pieces of software because they are "masked" behind the Microsoft Teams interface. One example of this is the Files tab in your team. In Figure 1-4, you can see that your documents all appear to be in Teams. However, they are really stored in SharePoint behind the scenes. We have elaborated this in Figure 1-4, which is similar to the meetings that are stored in Outlook. As a regular user, this isn't extremely important to know; however, if you are the administrator of a Microsoft Teams environment, these are key notes you want to be aware of because some of the maintenance and repairs that you perform might be done directly in that software, and not via Microsoft Teams.

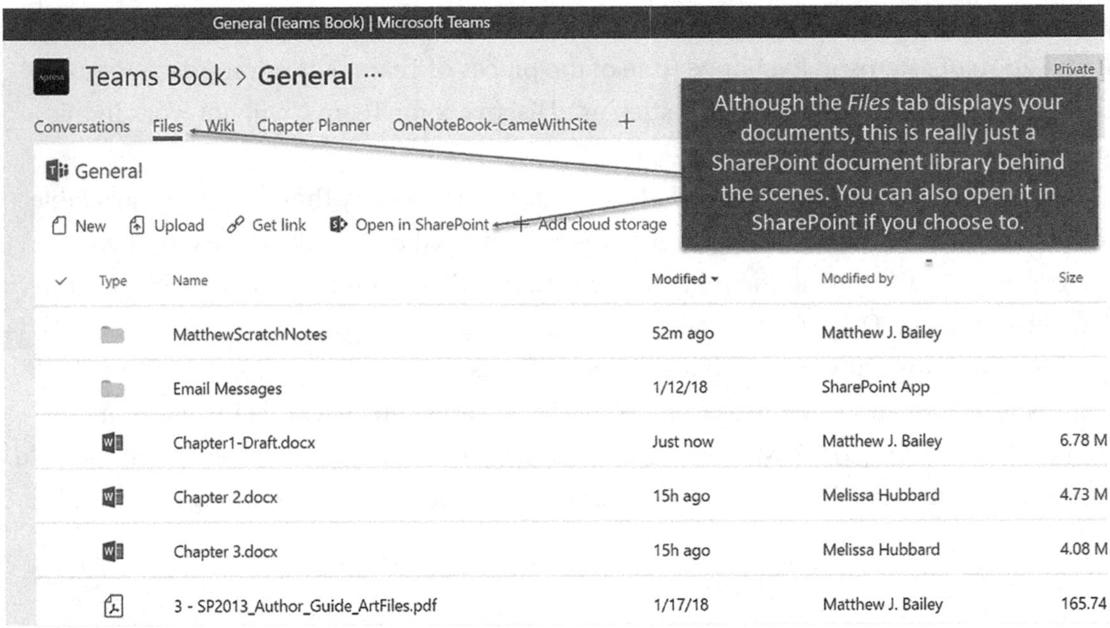

Figure 1-4. *An example of how the Microsoft Teams interface surfaces data from other applications so that it "appears" as though it is all in one place*

SharePoint and Teams

When creating a team, one of the components it creates is a Modern SharePoint Online Team Site with a document library. SharePoint Online must be active in your tenant to work with Microsoft Teams, because SharePoint On-Premises is not supported. The Shared Documents library is created inside this team for you; however, there are ways to use an existing document library from another SharePoint site if you currently have all of your documents somewhere else.

Note   Although each channel in Microsoft Teams has a corresponding folder in SharePoint Online for the files that you work with, the folder is not created until there is actually a file uploaded.

Some of the files that users upload are stored "behind the scenes" in this SharePoint document library. Figure 1-5 shows a SharePoint document library holding these documents. We go into where each file is stored later in this book.

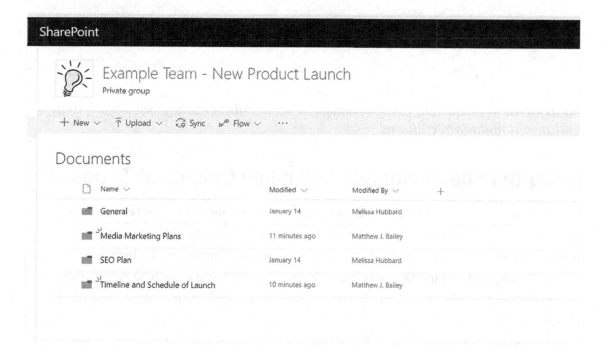

Figure 1-5. *A document library created in SharePoint Online from a team*

When a private channel is created, it will also provision a separate site collection with its own SharePoint document library with documents specific for users of that private channel allowing them to be kept separate from other members of the team.

If you open the document library in SharePoint, you will also be able to add metadata columns to provide additional information about the document such as a description or a status. These metadata columns will not be available to view within Teams at the current time.

Documents > **General**

	Name ∨	Modified ∨	Modified By ∨	Status ∨
📄	978-1-4842-3669-7_Ch1.docx	A few seconds ago	D'arce Hess	Completed
📄	978-1-4842-3669-7_Ch2.docx	A few seconds ago	D'arce Hess	In Progress
📄	978-1-4842-3669-7_Ch3.docx	May 4	D'arce Hess	
📄	978-1-4842-3669-7_Ch4.docx	May 4	D'arce Hess	
📄	978-1-4842-3669-7_Ch5.docx	May 4	D'arce Hess	
📄	978-1-4842-3669-7_Ch6.docx	A few seconds ago	D'arce Hess	Completed
📄	978-1-4842-3669-7_Ch7.docx	May 4	D'arce Hess	

Figure 1-6. *A document library created in SharePoint Online from a team with additional metadata columns*

Using the SharePoint Site Collection Outside of Teams

Whether or not we should encourage people to use the SharePoint site collection for other reasons (workflows, lists, etc.) is a good question that depends on your own reasoning. At the moment, the only portion of the SharePoint site collection that automatically appears in Microsoft Teams is the Shared Documents folder. You can use other parts of SharePoint, but you have to add them as a link from a tab or by adding cloud storage.

One potential upside of using the SharePoint site collection outside of the Teams interface is that SharePoint has much greater granular security, and this is one way to overcome the current limitation of no channel-based security in Teams. The downside of this, however, is that you are opening both Microsoft Teams and SharePoint to manage different artifacts.

Caution   Although you can put other things into a SharePoint site collection to add to the channel tab for easy access, changing the channels' folder structure does **not** update the channels in Teams. It is important that you only create them from the Teams interface.

Groups and Teams

Office 365 Groups (or Modern Groups) places users into meaningful groupings that allow you to set notifications or security across many applications. Technically, an Office 365 group is an object in Azure Active Directory. It can have one or many members and be used across most Office 365 applications. For example, you may have a marketing department with salespeople working with them. You might create a group called Marketing, add all of the employees from that area to this group, and then add the group to the application(s) you are using. This is much easier to manage than repeatedly adding each user individually to each application for security and notifications.

The reason that Office 365 Groups matter in conjunction with Microsoft Teams is because an Office 365 group is the parent of a team. Whenever you create a new team, it creates an Office 365 group (unless you select to create a team from an existing Office 365 group). You also choose whether the team is private or public (the group is of this same type). But in either case, behind the scenes, there is a group at a higher level that controls your team's security and other features. The relationship between Office 365 Groups and Teams becomes far more important later in the book as we dive into Teams administration. The Office 365 group is where the team's security is managed. It controls the permissions for the team. In order to store your files, the SharePoint team site is provisioned, and your team's files are stored in a document library that exists within that SharePoint team site.

Like other Office 365 applications that Microsoft Teams interacts with, Exchange only enables all of its benefits when it is fully online in the Office 365 suite. Although you can use Exchange On-Premises or Exchange dedicated (legacy) with Microsoft Teams, some functionality works and some does not. As a note, users hosted on Exchange Online or Exchange Dedicated vNext have access to all the features in Microsoft Teams.

The key takeaway is that Microsoft Teams uses Exchange to create a group mailbox that stores the team's information, such as meetings (messages are stored in a SharePoint folder). To see which functionalities are enabled or disabled (this depends on your version of Exchange), please visit the Microsoft website at `https://docs.microsoft.com/en-us/microsoftteams/exchange-teams-interact`.

Note   For the full Microsoft Teams experience, every user should be enabled for Exchange Online, SharePoint Online, and Office 365 Groups creation.

OneDrive for Business and Teams

OneDrive for Business is used a bit within Microsoft Teams. Mostly, it is where files that are shared from a team chat are stored (not a channel conversation). Permissions to the files are restricted automatically so that only the intended user can access them.

Summary

This chapter explained Microsoft Teams and the history of the platform and reviewed its core functionality. In the next chapter, we take a look at the components and how we get work done within a team.

CHAPTER 2

Working in Teams

Teams and their channels are the heart of user collaboration and productivity. Although Microsoft Teams can be used just for chatting and holding meetings, the true power of the application is recognized by adding teams and channels and knowing how to retrieve information from them. This chapter provides information and instructions on how to maximize working with Microsoft Teams. We explore creating teams, channels, and tabs, as well as searching by using the @commands and shortcuts.

What you can and cannot do in Microsoft Teams is based on the permission role you have. There are currently three roles available in Teams:

- Team member
- Team owner
- Guest (must be enabled by your administrator)

By default, anyone within an organization can create a team. When they do, they become the team owner. In Table 2-1, you see what default actions team members and team owners have the ability to do when working in Teams. Some of these default actions can also be modified by the team owner.

Note Guests are people that are not part of an organization and therefore do not have any corporate identity.

© Melissa Hubbard, Matthew J. Bailey, D'arce Hess, Mårten Hellebro 2021
M. Hubbard et al., *Mastering Microsoft Teams*, https://doi.org/10.1007/978-1-4842-6898-8_2

Table 2-1. *Default Owner and Team Member Settings in a New Team*

Action	Team Member	Team Owner	Guest
Creating a team		X	
Editing a team		X	
Deleting a team		X	
Adding team members		X	
Adding a channel	X	X	
Editing a channel	X	X	
Deleting a channel	X	X	
Creating a private channel	X	X	
Deleting a private channel	X		
Editing private channel name/description		N/A	
Getting channel email	X	X	X
Getting channel link	X	X	X
Favoriting a channel	X	X	X
Following a channel	X	X	X
Managing channels	X	X	
Uploading files	X	X	X
Deleting files	X	X	X
Downloading files	X	X	X
Adding tabs	X	X	
Deleting tabs	X	X	
Adding connectors	X	X	
Adding Apps	X	X	

Note   Team owners may restrict who can add apps to a team. Some apps may require additional permissions to be installed or licensing.

Teams

Teams are a central location where a group of people with common work functions can hold conversations, collaborate on content, and create work products. Teams are the container for channels and tabs. The first step to setting up a team is creating the team itself; then, you can build upon the functionality by adding channels, tabs, and connectors. Let's get started!

Note   Users must be enabled for Office 365 Groups to create teams in Microsoft Teams.

Creating a Team

To create a team

1. Click **Add team**, located on the bottom left in the Teams app, as seen in Figure 2-1.

2. Click the **Create team** button.

3. Enter a team name, description, and privacy settings.

4. Add team members. A person's name, distribution list, or mail-enabled security group can be selected.

Figure 2-1. *Creating a team*

Be sure to name your team something meaningful. Although it is optional, it is recommended to enter a description for the team. As more and more teams are added, a description helps people in the organization determine which public team they should join.

You also need to decide on the privacy for the new team. If you don't change the setting, it defaults to private. This means that only team owners can add team members. There is also the option to make a team public, which means that anyone in the organization that has a Microsoft Teams license can join.

Note   It is important to make sure that a team with the name that you plan to use does not already exist. Nothing stops you from creating a name that is the same as another team; however, doing so can create confusion and other issues for your users.

Another option is to create a team from an existing Office 365 group. When creating a new team, first, click the link at the bottom of the window that says Join or create a team. Next, click the *Create a team* button. A window will then appear with a link to select titled *Create a team from an existing Office 365 group*. You are given a list of groups you are the owner of to choose from. Once you select the group, you can create the team. Everyone that is part of the group is added as members of the team.

Note   Teams can be reordered in the left navigation by dragging and dropping them where you want them. The channels that are part of the team are moved with it.

Managing a Team

When you create a new team, there are only a limited number of options available to configure its settings. Much of this is done by using the **Manage team** option. Within this area of a team, you have the option to change the overall settings for everyone on the team. This includes setting the overall permissions for what internal and guest users can do. You can also determine whether @mentions and fun stuff like emojis or animated GIFs can be used and change the team picture (icon).

Let's review how to add a team picture:

1.   Click the ellipse (...) to the right of the team name, and then select **Manage team**.

2.   Select the Settings tab, and then select the team picture. Expand the section. Click the **Change picture** link and select the picture. In the pop-up box, locate the image that you want to use.

3.   Click the **Save** button.

Editing a Team

Situations may arise when there is a need to change the name or description of a team, such as an organizational change, another team in your organization with the same name, or team member feedback.

To edit a team name

1. Click the ellipse (...) to the right of the team name, and then select
   Edit team, as seen in Figure 2-2.

2. Change the team name, description, and privacy settings as
   desired.

3. Click the **Done** button.

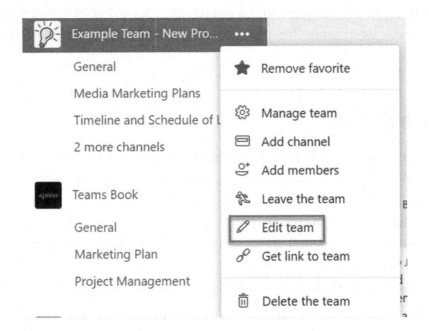

Figure 2-2. *Editing a team name, privacy setting, or description*

Adding Team Members

Team owners have the ability to add team members to both private and public teams.

To add team members

1. Click the ellipse (...) to the right of the name, and then select
   Add members, as seen in Figure 2-3.

2. Begin typing the name of the person, distribution list, or
   mail-enabled security group that you wish to add to the team.

3. Click **Add**.

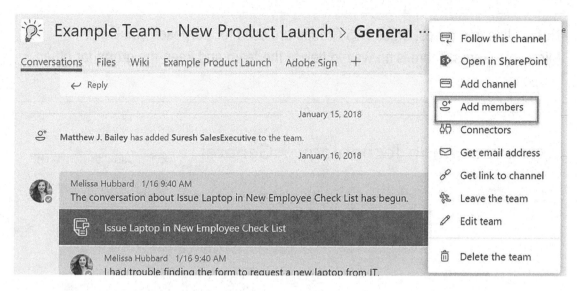

Figure 2-3. *Adding team members*

The people that you add will receive a notification email that they have been added to the team.

Deleting a Team

When a team is deleted, all the channels, chat, files, and the Office 365 group are deleted. When the team is deleted, it is held in the tenant's "recycle bin" in Azure Active Directory (AAD) for 30 days and referred to as being in a "soft-delete" status. During this time, the team can be restored using PowerShell, which requires the assistance of an administrator. It can take up to 24 hours for a deleted team to reappear after being restored. After 30 days have passed without being restored, however, the team is permanently deleted in the environment and cannot be recovered by anyone, including Microsoft.

To delete a team

1. Click the ellipse (...) to the right of the team name, and then select
    Delete the team, as seen in Figure 2-4.

2. Click the box stating that you understand that everything is
    deleted.

3. Click the **Delete team** button.

Note   In some cases, Office 365 Groups are used for purposes outside of Microsoft Teams. There is no way to delete the team and keep the group for other purposes.

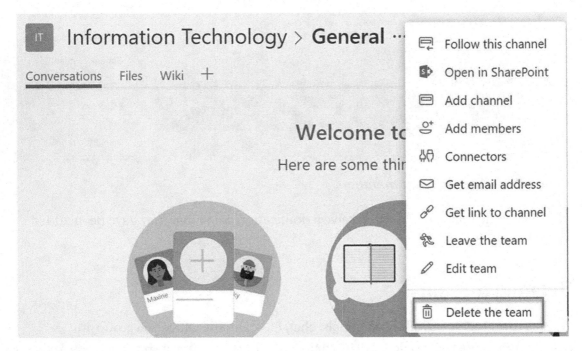

Figure 2-4. *Deleting a team*

Channels

Channels within a team provide a means to separate content and conversations for different projects, subjects, organizations, or disciplines. One organization we worked with created a separate team for every IT project. Within those teams, they created channels for different work functions on the project, such as development, quality assurance, and project management.

When viewing teams, the channels fall underneath them in the application navigation. Every person that is part of a team can access every channel, as in the example shown in Figure 2-5.

Figure 2-5. *A team with channels in the left navigation*

Adding a Channel

By default, every person that is part of a team can create a channel for that team. Whenever a team is created, it automatically comes with a General channel. This channel should be used for team conversations and content related to the overall goals and objectives. When there is a need to collaborate and discuss something more specific, it is recommended to create a new channel. Before creating a channel, it is important to make sure that there is not already a channel being used for your planned topic. In Chapter 6, we discuss appropriate reasons to create a channel.

To add a channel

1. Click the ellipse (...) to the right of the team name, and then select **Add channel**, as seen in Figure 2-6.

2. Provide a name and a description for the channel.

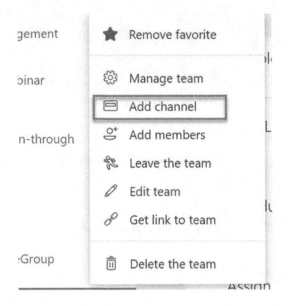

Figure 2-6. *Adding a channel*

When prompted to provide a name, be sure to name your channel something meaningful. Although it is optional, it is recommended to enter a description for the channel. As a team grows and more channels are added, descriptions help team members determine where they should have conversations and collaborate. A meaningful channel name and description can also avoid duplication of channels. If the name is unrecognizable and there is no description, another team member may create a channel that contains similar content and conversations.

Adding a Private Channel

Private channels provide a collaboration space for a special subset of members from the Team. Both team owners and team members can create a private channel. The team member who creates the private channel becomes the owner of the private channel. Only the owner of the private channel can add members to the private channel. Private channels can be identified by the lock icon to the left of the title.

To add a channel

1.   Click the ellipse (…) to the right of the team name, and then select **Add channel**, as seen in Figure 2-7.

2. Provide a name and a description for the channel.

3. Select **Private** from the Privacy drop-down menu.

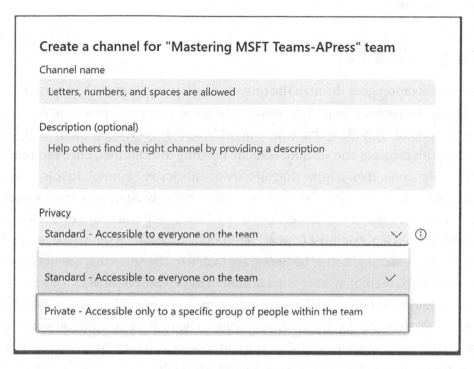

Figure 2-7. *Adding a channel*

Note   In order to add a person to a private channel, the person must already be a member of Team. You cannot add users outside of your Team to join only a channel at this time.

Editing a Channel

As the content and conversations evolve within a channel, there may be a need to change the name or description of the channel.

To edit the channel name or description

1. Click the ellipse (...) next to the channel name, and then click **Edit this channel**.

2. Change the channel name or description and if the channel should automatically show for all members.

3. Click **Save**.

Deleting a Channel

While an organization goes through the process of adopting Microsoft Teams, the need to delete a channel is bound to come up. Since any member of a team can create a channel by default, it is likely that someone will accidently create a channel or experiment with creating one without actually needing the channel. For example, a channel may be created for a topic that already has an active channel. In this case, the channel with the least amount of content should be deleted. Another circumstance that leads to deletion is when the channel limit is reached. There can only be as many as 200 channels for each team. For most teams, 200 channels should be more than enough, but if the limit is approaching, it may be necessary to delete channels that are not being used often or at all. Each team may have a maximum of 30 private channels.

When a channel is deleted, all conversations and tabs are deleted along with the channel. The channel can be restored, but it cannot be re-created with the same name as a blank slate. What this means is that you can restore a channel you deleted, but you cannot reuse the name of a channel you deleted again later.

To delete a channel

1. Click the ellipse (...) next to the channel name, and then click **Delete this channel**.

2. Click the **Delete** button, as seen in Figure 2-8.

Figure 2-8. File link when deleting a channel

When you delete a channel, you are provided a link to the folder where channel files are located. Since the files are stored in SharePoint, they are not deleted when the channel is deleted.

To delete channel files

1. Navigate to the *General* channel, and select the *Files* tab.

2. Click **Open in SharePoint**. This opens the team document library in your Internet browser showing a view of the channel folder.

3. Click **Documents** to the left of the channel name.

4. Click the check mark to the left of the channel name folder, and then click **Delete**.

Note   When a channel is deleted, it will remain in a recycle bin for 30 days. During these 30 days, it will still be counted against the 200-channel limit. This also includes the 30-private-channel limit.

Restoring a Channel

If a deleted channel needs to be restored, this can be done quickly with the restore channel functionality.

To restore a channel

1. Click the ellipse (...) to the right of the team name, and then select **Manage team**.

2. Select the Channels tab. If any channels have been deleted, they show up in the deleted section.

3. Click **Restore**.

Channel Email

Every channel comes with an email address. When the channel is emailed, it creates a new conversation thread in Teams. The email address of the person that emailed the channel is shown at the top of the conversation. The subject of the email appears in bold letters; this is followed by the email body. There is also a link to the original email, which is accessible to anyone in the organization but not external guests. When that link is clicked, it opens the email in Outlook. If the user is not logged in to Outlook, they are prompted to do so. All email messages are saved in a subfolder called Emails in the channel folder.

This channel email functionality is meant to deter important messages from being lost in endless email threads. Often, people miss information when someone forgets to Reply All when responding to an email or forwards it to someone else. The channel email helps avoid these blunders. Additionally, when new team members come aboard, it is much easier to get them up to speed when they can read through conversations in a channel.

To get the channel email address

1. Click the ellipse (...) to the right of the channel name, and then click **Get email address**.

2. Click the **Copy** button, as seen in Figure 2-9.

Get email address

See advanced settings for more options.

hannel - Mastering MSFT Teams-APress <a9872c0a.cloudway.no@emea.teams.ms>

🗑 Remove email address

Close	Copy

Figure 2-9. *Channel email address*

The email address is displayed along with links to advanced settings and to remove the email address. The email address is generated by the system and cannot be changed. The Copy button can quickly capture the email address to paste into an email.

You can control who can send an email to the channel email address by clicking the advanced settings link. By default, anyone—even people who are not a member of the team or the organization—can send an email to a channel email address. You can choose to have only team members able to email the channel email address or to have emails only sent from certain domains. Examples of email domains are @hotmail.com, @gmail.com, @noteworthytt.com, and @melihubb.com.

If the **Remove email address** button is clicked, the email address is disabled. If anyone tries to email the channel once an email address is removed, they will receive a delivery failure.

Note   If the channel email address is removed, it cannot be recovered. Only remove the email if you are absolutely sure you do not want the channel email address functionality.

Channel Link

In some instances, you may want to refer a channel to someone that hasn't yet adopted Microsoft Teams and doesn't know what a channel is or how to find one. Also, members of an organization may be part of several teams, and each team may have many channels. In this case, you can simply provide a team member a link to the channel, and they can paste it into an Internet browser. They are then prompted to open the channel in the Teams app, if they have it installed, or they can view the channel within the browser. If someone who is not a member of the team tries to use the link, they will not be able to access the channel.

To get the channel link

1. Click the ellipse (…) to the right of the channel name, and then click **Get a link to the channel**.

2. Click the **Copy** button, as seen in Figure 2-10.

Get a link to the channel

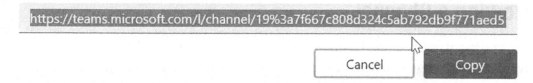

Figure 2-10. Channel link

Favoriting a Channel

To keep up with the conversations and content in a channel, team members have the ability to favorite and follow channels. When a channel is favorited, the member sees the channel name in the list under the team name. If a channel is not favorited, the member needs to click more channels underneath the last favorited channel in the list to view it. When a channel is @mentioned in a conversation, all members that have it favorited receive a notification. @mentions is discussed in Chapter 3. By default, when a member is added to a team, the five most active channels are automatically favorited. If there are fewer than five channels, any new channels are automatically added as favorites when they are created, until there are five.

To favorite a channel

1. Click the arrow next to **more channels** underneath the team name, as seen in Figure 2-11.

2. Click the star to the right of the channel name.

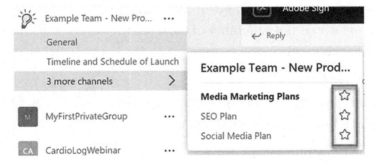

Figure 2-11. *Favoriting a channel*

Following a Channel

When a channel is followed, the member receives a notification whenever a new conversation message is added. There is also an activity feed in which members can view all recent conversations in the channels they are following. It is recommended that a member only follow the channels that have the most importance to them. Depending on how active a channel is, a lot of notifications may be sent out. If a member follows too many channels, they may begin to ignore the notifications all together, which render them useless.

To follow a channel

1. Click the ellipse (...) next to the channel name, and then click
    Follow this channel, as seen in Figure 2-12.

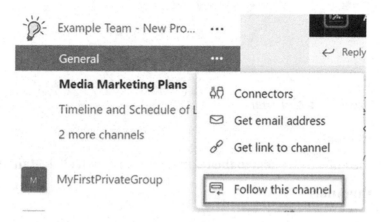

Figure 2-12. *Following a channel*

Note   The activity feed shows team members all activity of channels they follow
as well as mentions of them or any team or channel they are part of. It shows
them replies to their conversation messages and likes of the message. All saved
conversation messages are also shown. More about mentions and liking messages
can be found in Chapter 3.

Managing Channels

There is a way to view and manage all **channels** for a team in one view. You can see
the channel names and descriptions along with the number of people that follow the
channel as seen in Figure 2-13. You can also see the date that the channel had its last
activity. If the last activity occurred on the current day, you can see how many hours ago
the activity was.

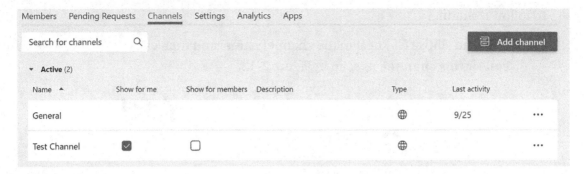

Figure 2-13. *Managing channels*

To manage channels

1. Click the ellipse (…) next to the team name, and then click **Manage team**.

2. Click **Channels**.

Pinning a Channel

Pinning a channel allows for you to provide a focused area for channels that you may be the most active in without needing to navigate to the Team. The pinned channels will appear above your Teams.

To pin a channel

1. Click the ellipse (…) next to the channel name, and then click **Pin.**

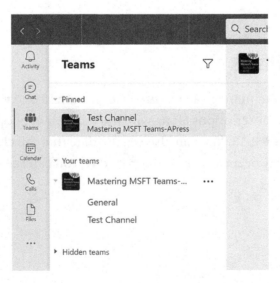

Figure 2-14. *Pinned channels*

Tabs

Tabs make the customizable workspace within Microsoft Teams possible. Tabs are containers within a team's channels that hold content connected to a cloud-based service, such as what's seen in Figure 2-15. Files, websites, SharePoint lists and libraries, Planner tasks, Power BI reports, and even third-party cloud-based tools can be viewed and worked on in tabs. Every channel has its own set of tabs that can be configured. There are three tabs that come automatically with every channel: Posts, Files, and Wiki. The Wiki tab can be deleted, but the Posts and Files tabs cannot be deleted because they are part of core Microsoft Teams functionality.

Figure 2-15. *Tabs in a team*

Note   If you want to focus on working in just one tab, you can expand and view it without the teams and channels list on the left part of the app or the tabs and team name at the top of the app.

Posts Tab

Every channel within a team has a separate Posts tab. The conversations that occur in the channels cannot be viewed together. In other words, you cannot view all team conversations from every channel in one view. Figure 2-16 provides an example. Conversations are discussed further in Chapter 3.

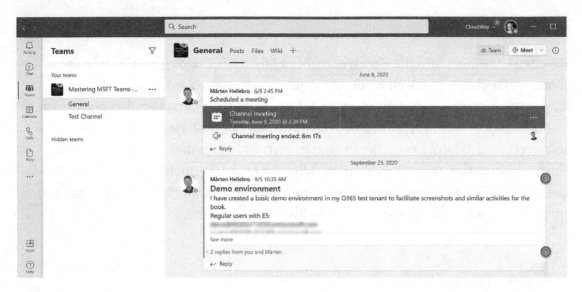

Figure 2-16. *Post tab*

Files Tab

The Files tab is where documents and other files are uploaded for team members to collaborate and share. An example of this is shown in Figure 2-17.

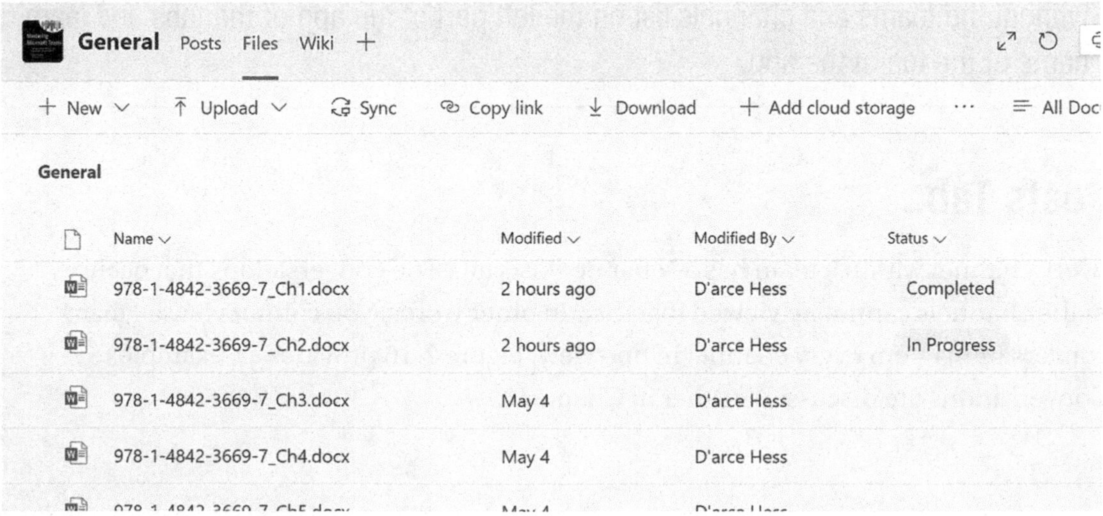

Figure 2-17. *Files tab*

Files should only be added if they pertain to the channel topic. The Files tab should not be used as a place to store personal files. It is different from the Posts tab in that all the files that are uploaded in the separate channel tabs live in one SharePoint document library for the team. Every channel gets a folder in the document library. When you click the Files tab in a channel, you get a view of the files in the Channel folder. The fields displayed are File type, Name, Modified, and Modified by. The modified field shows the date that the file was last changed. If this is within the current day, it shows the number of hours ago that the file was changed. The **Modified by** field shows which team member last changed the file.

Uploading Files

To upload a file to the Files tab

1. Click **Upload**.

2. Select the file or files that you want to upload.

3. Click **Open**.

Deleting Files

To delete a file from the Files tab

1. Click the document, which highlights it in blue.

2. Click **Delete**.

3. Click **Confirm**.

Note   When a file is removed from the Files tab, it is moved to the SharePoint recycle bin.

Downloading Files

To download a file from the Files tab

1. Click the document, which highlights it in blue.

2. Click **Download**. The downloaded files folder opens.

3. Select the file, and then click **Open**.

Wiki Tab

The Wiki tab as seen in Figure 2-18 quickly captures ideas and information on one central page per channel. The Wiki tab is comprised of pages and sections. When you add pages, they are displayed in a navigation pane on the left. When sections are added to a page, they appear in the navigation underneath the page that they are a part of, thus creating a table of contents–like functionality.

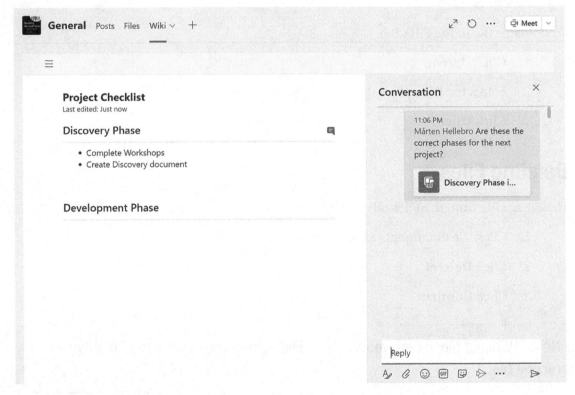

Figure 2-18. *The Wiki tab in a team displaying a conversation*

Organizations can use the wiki page to present information, such as a checklist or the steps of a process. If you create a section for each checklist item, team members can use the built-in conversations functionality to discuss the process and provide feedback. For example, if you create a wiki page for a checklist of things that need to happen when a new employee joins a project, new team members can add comments and make suggestions. All of this happens within the wiki page. The conversations appear within the wiki page, but they are also added under a channel's Posts tab for visibility. A conversation message includes a link that brings team members to the wiki page. If someone responds to a conversation in the Posts tab, it is also displayed in the conversation in the wiki section associated with it. There is also the ability to add additional wiki tabs to a channel.

On the back end, the wiki content is stored in the same SharePoint site collection that is created when you create a team. First, all the wiki content for that channel is placed in a document library titled Teams Wiki Data (see Figure 2-19). This folder is automatically created by the system when you create your first wiki page.

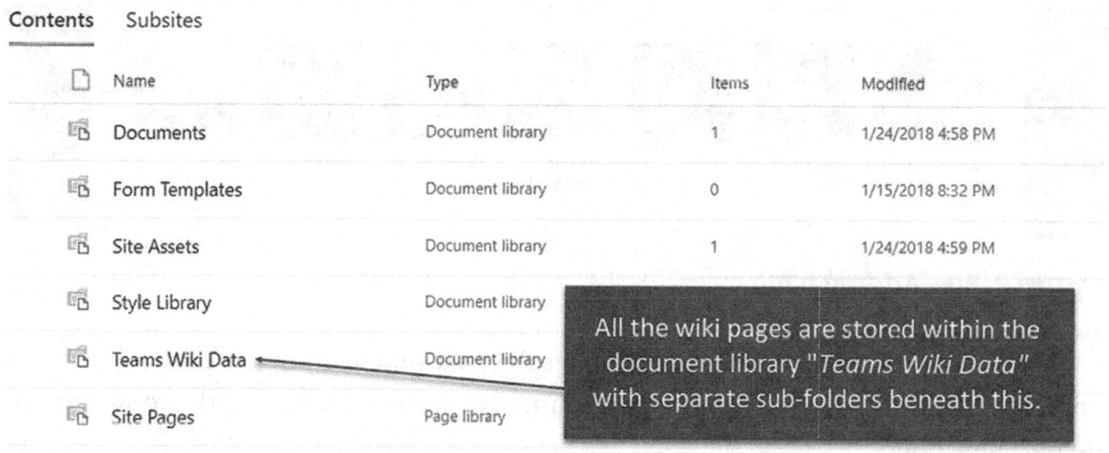

Figure 2-19. *The Teams Wiki Data document library within your SharePoint site collection*

Within the Teams Wiki Data folder, there is another subfolder for each channel. Inside of each of these subfolders are the system files for each wiki. Each wiki page is stored as a .mht file, making it best to only edit wikis within Microsoft Teams and not via the SharePoint document library.

Adding a Tab

To create a tab

1. Click the plus sign that is located to the far right of the tabs area of the channel.

2. Select the connector or app for the service that you want to connect to and use in the tab, as seen in Figure 2-20.

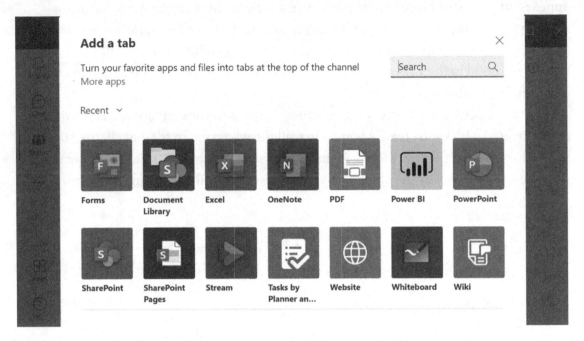

Figure 2-20. *Adding a tab*

The connector that you select determines the next step in adding the tab. Depending on what you select, you are prompted to select a file or a work product, or to create a new one.

Note   For information to be secure when adding a website to a tab, the URL needs to start with https.

Deleting a Tab

To delete a tab

1. Click the name of the tab that you want to delete.

2. Click the drop-down arrow, and then select **Remove**, as seen in Figure 2-21.

3. Click **Remove** when prompted.

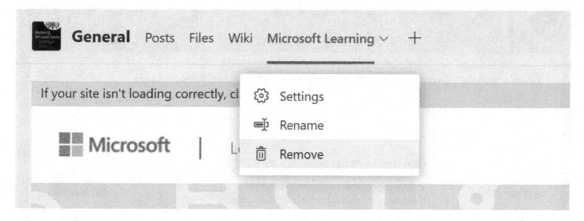

Figure 2-21. *Removing a tab*

The tab is deleted, but that does not mean that the file or work product displayed is deleted from the source.

Connectors

Connectors are a gateway to cloud services that Microsoft Teams can interact with. The connectors are contained within tabs in the channel. Microsoft Teams connects with many Office 365 apps, such as Planner, Excel, and OneNote. Third-party services—such as Trello, Twitter, GitHub, and Smartsheet—can also be connected. It is possible to create custom connectors using a web hook. You can learn more about developing custom connectors from Microsoft's website.

Note   If the team member who created a connector is removed from the team, the connector stops working until another teammate re-creates it.

To add a connector

1. Click the ellipse (...) next to the channel name, and then click **Connectors**.

2. Search for the service of choice, and then click the **Configure** button, as seen in Figure 2-22.

3. Log in to the service.

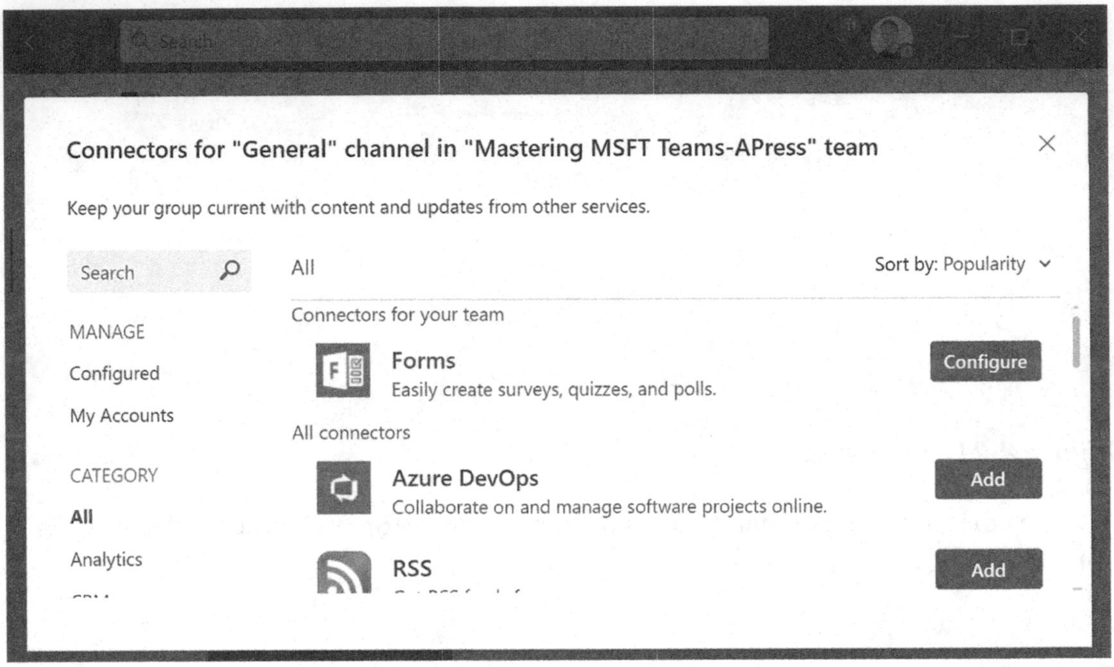

Figure 2-22. *Adding a connector*

It is important to remember that a connector is a connection to another service that can read and write data to and from your organization. In a way, this a great benefit: you do not have to leave the Microsoft Teams client. Your administrators might find it to be a data or security risk, however. In the Office 365 administration center, you can disable or enable each connector separately so that only the options vetted for your organization can be used.

Search

Searching in Microsoft Teams is a bit basic, although there are some filtering options available. If you are used to a rich, sortable, minutely refined search experience such as what exists in SharePoint, unfortunately, you will not find that in Microsoft Teams yet. You need to search to find the files that you work with, so let's review the options that are available and go over how to use them to best extent possible.

The search experience begins with a combined search and command bar, as seen in Figure 2-23. It is rather self-explanatory: you just type what you are searching for. This performs a broad search across all of your teams. The results are returned within one or more of the following filtering categories:

- Messages

- People

- Files

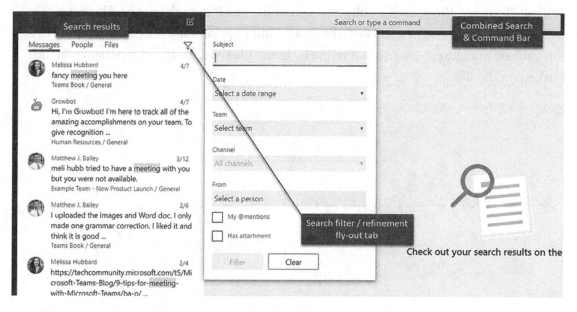

Figure 2-23. *The search experience in Microsoft Teams*

The Messages category returns results from your private chats, channel conversations that are posted for all to see within a team channel, conversations you have with bots, and emails sent to a team.

It does not return the results from the wiki, meeting titles, or documents in your Files tab, such as OneDrive for Business, Dropbox, or Google Drive.

The People category is used to find persons within your organization. If you want to find data from a specific person, you want to use the Filter tab.

The Files tab returns Word, Excel, PowerPoint, and OneNote files, images, text files, and PDFs. Teams returns the results of the search term, which appears within the filename or within the body of text. It also searches within .zip files for contents containing your search phrase.

Note   Content Search allows you to search across most of the components of Teams, including Exchange, SharePoint, and OneDrive for Business. It is only available to administrators using the Office 365 administration center.

Using the Search Filter

As teams and the amount of content grows larger, attempting to find content can be difficult. To refine the search results, you can utilize the Filter tab (pane). The Filter tab only appears in Messages and Files (there is no filter option for the People category). As you can see in Figure 2-24, you can refine by team, file type, and/or the person who last worked on the file.

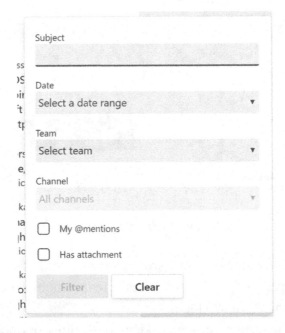

Figure 2-24.   *The Filter tab in search alters, depending on which category you have highlighted*

Search for Messages Within Teams

You can search for terms within a chat or channel.

To search for a term within a chat or channel

1.   Use **Ctrl+F** (**cmd+F** on macOS).

2.   Enter the term you want to search for and press **Enter**.

All of your results will appear from within the chat or channel conversation.

Figure 2-25. *Search from your location*

Search for Teams and Channels

To search for a team or a channel by its name, type the name of the team or channel into the command box. The search will bring suggestions in a drop-down to help you find the team or channel you are looking for.

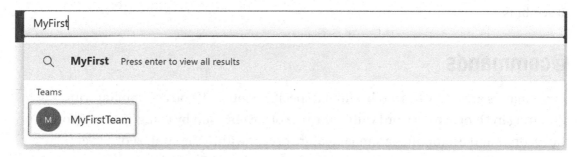

Figure 2-26. *Search for a team or channel*

How to Use Search Modifiers

As with many search engines, you can use search modifiers to help narrow your search from the beginning. The following are a few of the popular search modifiers that you may want to use:

- From:Person's name

- In:Channel or group chat name

- Subject:keyword from a channel message with a subject line

- Sent:Date

Note   Use a [partial term]* to find all results with a matching prefix such as *Mes and you would get all results that included Mes such as message and messenger.

Quick Commands and the Command Bar

The command bar is combined with the search box. Quick commands are shortcuts that perform an action or return some type of data. Quick commands start with / or @ symbols.

@commands

@commands are a way to search within a specific context. If you are familiar with searching in Google for a word within the title of a web result by using Title:MyWord, the @command exemplifies a similar feature except within the context of a user (like @mentioning someone on Twitter) or within the context of an installed app. By typing the @ symbol, you receive a list of users and apps that you can use the @command with. In Figure 2-28, we used the @Weather command.

Figure 2-27. *Using the @ command in the command bar*

After selecting the @Weather command, the command bar then prefaces any search you perform with the Weather app. You are now able to search for the weather in cities across the world (see Figure 2-28).

Figure 2-28. *Selecting a city to use with the @Weather command to return the current weather for that city*

> **Note**   If you use an @command for an app that you do not have installed, you are prompted to install the app.

/commands

Slash commands (/commands), or shortcuts, in the command bar provide another way to quickly perform a task or obtain data. At the time we write this book, there are less than 20 slash commands available to users. It is highly likely that this number will increase as Microsoft Teams grows in popularity. The following is a list of available slash commands:

- /activity – View a team member's activity
- /available – Changes your team's status to Available
- /away – Changes your team's status to Away
- /busy – Changes your team's status to Busy
- /call – Initiate a call
- /dnd – Changes your team's status to Do Not Disturb
- /files – See your recent files
- /goto – Go to a certain team or channel
- /help – Get help (with Teams; not the "lie on the couch" kind)
- /join – Join a team
- /keys – View keyboard shortcuts
- /mentions – See all of your mentions (Handy if your team's channels are really busy!)
- /org – View an org chart (yours or someone else's)
- /saved – View your saved list
- /unread – See all of your unread activity
- /whatsnew – Check out what's new in Teams
- /who – Ask Who (a new app that lets you search for people by name or topic) a question

The following covers some of the more popular slash commands.

/activity

/activity helps you find data when you can't remember exactly what a file is called, but you do remember who worked on it last. It can also come in handy if someone left your project, and you want to see what they were working on recently so that you can reassign it to someone else.

/dnd, /busy, /away, /available

/dnd, /busy, /away, and /available offer quick and easy ways to change your notification status. Although it may take a couple of seconds, these commands change the colored icon next to your name to alert others of your availability. The /dnd command sets your status to Do Not Disturb and automatically forwards calls to your voice mail. The other three slash commands provide a visual indicator that indicates whether you are available or not. These commands do not prevent someone from calling or messaging you the way that the /dnd command does.

/who

The /who command triggers the Who Bot, which is used to find specific people (and more detailed information about them) within your organization. If you have not used it before, it prompts you to allow it to perform searches on your behalf. An example of this experience is seen in Figure 2-29.

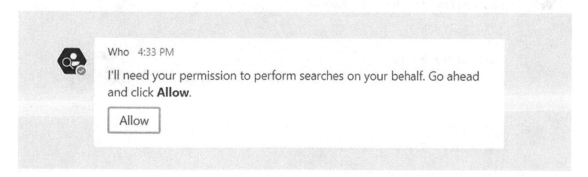

Figure 2-29. *The Who Bot asking for permission to search on your behalf*

If for some reason more than one result returns, you are prompted to select the result that you are searching for (see Figure 2-30).

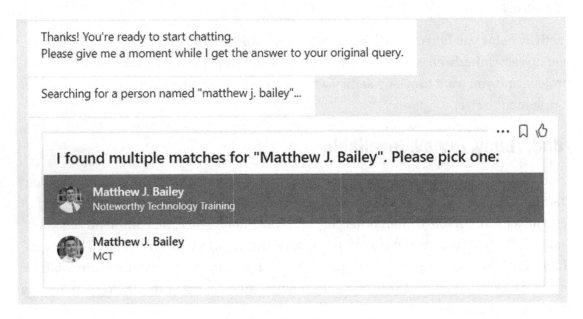

Figure 2-30. *Displays the results from the Who Bot if you receive more than one result*

After selecting the correct person that you want to inquire about, a *card* displays more information about the user, as seen in Figure 2-31.

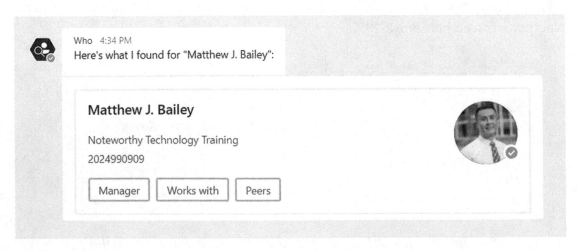

Figure 2-31. *A card with information about the person you are searching for*

From here, you can find activity-based information, such as who the person works with, their manager, and their peers. This can be helpful if the person is out on leave, for example, and you need to find someone who is able to assist you with the responsibilities this person normally has. It can also be used to learn the person's level of management before you engage in conversation with them, since there is usually an expectation of treating higher-level executives in a formal manner.

There are many other slash commands available in Teams to accelerate your workload. Feel free to experiment with them yourself.

Tips

As we wrap up this chapter on how to work efficiently in Microsoft Teams, let's discuss a few quick tips on how to improve your working experience even further.

Keyboard Shortcuts

First, let's discuss keyboard shortcuts. You can see all of the available shortcuts by pressing **ALT+/** on your keyboard. After doing so, you should see something similar to what's shown in Figure 2-32.

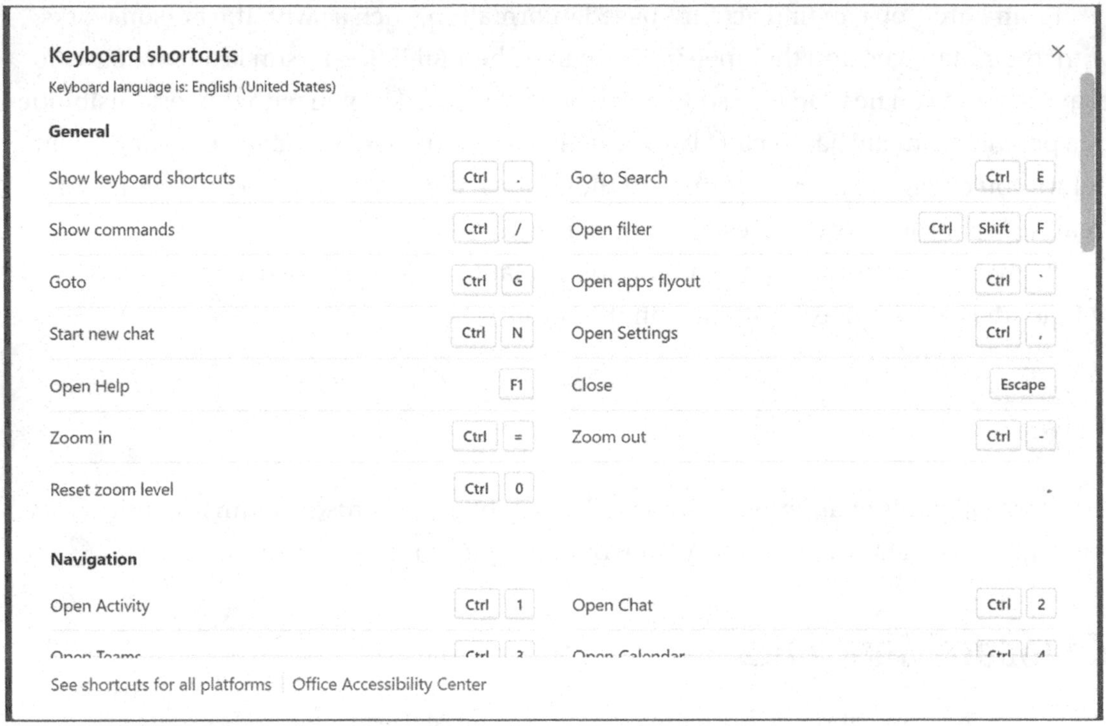

Keyboard shortcuts   ✕

Keyboard language is: English (United States)

General

Show keyboard shortcuts	`Ctrl` `.`	Go to Search	`Ctrl` `E`
Show commands	`Ctrl` `/`	Open filter	`Ctrl` `Shift` `F`
Goto	`Ctrl` `G`	Open apps flyout	`Ctrl` `` ` ``
Start new chat	`Ctrl` `N`	Open Settings	`Ctrl` `,`
Open Help	`F1`	Close	`Escape`
Zoom in	`Ctrl` `=`	Zoom out	`Ctrl` `-`
Reset zoom level	`Ctrl` `0`		

Navigation

Open Activity	`Ctrl` `1`	Open Chat	`Ctrl` `2`
Open Teams	`Ctrl` `3`	Open Calendar	`Ctrl` `4`

See shortcuts for all platforms   Office Accessibility Center

Figure 2-32. A listing of the shortcut keys available in Microsoft Teams

Some of these keyboard shortcuts are available in Windows, and some of them are specific to Teams and Skype for Business. Feel free to experiment with them to see which ones work best for you.

Ctrl+K (Adding a Link)

Although there are keys to add attachments, animated GIFs, start a meeting, and change the fonts in a conversation, there isn't a button to add a hyperlink. By pressing Ctrl+K on the keyboard, you can quickly add a link to the text you are typing. As seen in Figure 2-33, you can type the display text and the URL that the link goes to. We use this often by creating statements such as, "Please find the document to review **here**."

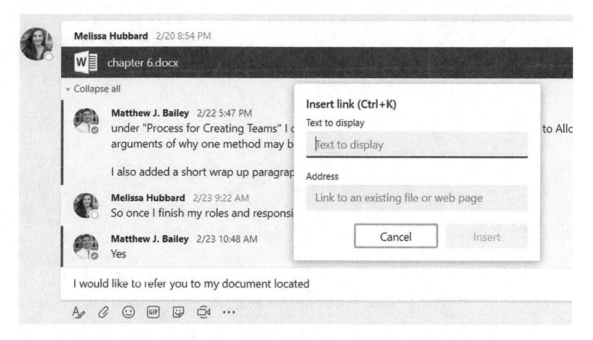

Figure 2-33. *Adding a link to a channel conversation by selecting Ctrl+K*

Summary

We have now reviewed the components inside a team that enable you to complete your work. We have explored channels, tabs, and connectors. We investigated different ways to retrieve data with search, @commands, and keyboard shortcuts. Now let's continue our journey by learning about the different ways to communicate within Teams.

CHAPTER 3

Communicating in Teams

Microsoft Teams offers a suite of communication tools that empower team members to be engaged and collaborative with one another. In the modern world, team members are on the go, work from home, or are in remote locations away from their team. Having reliable virtual communication options is absolutely essential to drive productivity by working together and making decisions, both with colleagues inside the organization and with external contacts that can easily be invited as guests into a team and participate in the collaboration as a teammate. In this chapter, we'll discuss voice, video, imagery, channel conversation, chat, and other ways to communicate in Microsoft Teams.

But we need to start with one of the most important aspects of Microsoft Teams, how to manage your notifications.

Notifications in Microsoft Teams

Notifications are a great way to stay up to date with everything that is important to you in Microsoft Teams. And at the same time, it can be somewhat overwhelming with too many notifications, and it is easy to miss the most relevant ones.

To fine-tune your Teams notification settings to suit your preferences is essential; notification settings are not controlled by IT, so it's up to you to find an assortment of settings that work for you.

© Melissa Hubbard, Matthew J. Bailey, D'arce Hess, Mårten Hellebro 2021
M. Hubbard et al., *Mastering Microsoft Teams*, https://doi.org/10.1007/978-1-4842-6898-8_3

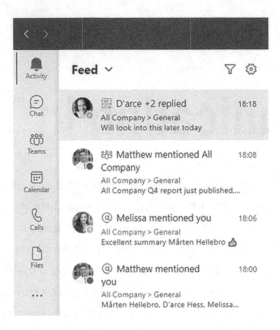

Figure 3-1. *Notifications showed in the Activity feed in Microsoft Teams*

General Notification Settings

The general notification settings are found by selecting your picture in the top right-hand corner in Teams.

Here, you will find notification settings for mentions, replies, chats, and meetings together with an option to play sound for notifications. With security in mind, you can choose to not display a message preview in the banner to eliminate the risk of revealing sensitive information to others looking at your screen.

An email can be sent with a summary of all missed activity, you decide how often it will be sent, or you can select to turn it off completely. This can be useful if you are a member of multiple Teams organizations at the same time and therefore can't stay up to date in all places all the time.

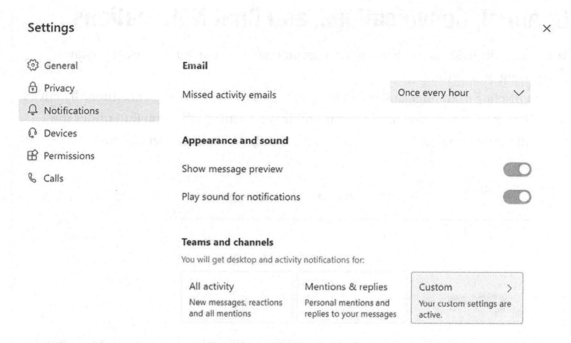

Figure 3-2. *Notification settings in detail*

There are two types of notifications:

- **Banner** is the small window "popping up" from the taskbar, sometimes referred to as a "toaster," meant to draw your attention to something important.

- **Show in feed** – notifications will be shown in the Activity feed found at the top left-hand side corner in Teams. The activity feed is also where all notifications and alerts are displayed, as seen in Figure 3-1.

Note   It is important that you find the notification settings that work for you, for mentions, replies, chats, and meetings, and it is not a universal setting that suits everyone. Also, note that there is a difference between these notification settings and those found in the Teams mobile app, which you can read about in the following.

Channel, Conversations, and Chat Notifications

You can set individual notification settings on channels, conversations, and chats depending on relevance.

Right-click a channel, and select Channel notifications; now select either All activity or Off. Under Custom, you have similar notification settings that you find under the General notification settings (as seen in Figure 3-3), but specific per channel.

🔔 Channel notifications >	**All activity** Posts, replies, mentions
✣ Pin	
🔏 Hide	**Off** Except direct replies, personal mentions
⚙ Manage channel	**Custom**

Figure 3-3. *Control how you want to receive notifications for a specific channel*

If you are involved in an active conversation, but you don't want to receive any notifications about new messages, or you are very keen on not missing any new messages from another conversation, you can turn notifications on or off for individual conversations. Right-click the conversation, and select Turn off/on notifications, as seen in Figure 3-4.

Figure 3-4. *Stop receiving notifications for this specific conversation*

Chats and especially meeting chats can sometimes be quite chatty; it is a good thing you have two options to control the chat notifications for individual chats, as seen in Figure 3-5. Right-click a specific chat and select either

- Mute, to opt out from receiving notifications on new messages

or

- Leave, if you do not want to be part of the chat anymore

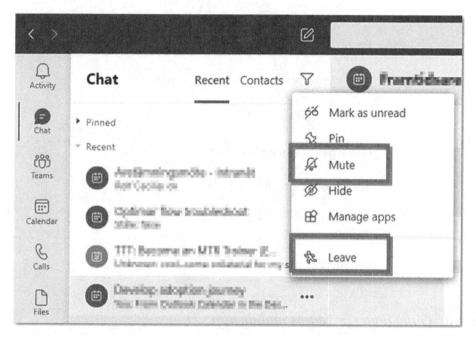

Figure 3-5. *Mute notifications for a chat or leave the chat to stop receiving messages*

Notifications on Teams Mobile App

Nowadays, many of us carry around our work mobiles all the time; we might even have them with us in the bedroom at night. How we choose to do work is up to each of us, but an important feature of the Teams mobile app is the ability to set quiet hours. With this feature enabled, you won't be disturbed by Teams notifications when you're not working.

When everyone in your organization has this feature enabled, all your team members can feel safe sending messages whatever time suits them, without feeling guilty about potentially disturbing someone outside of working hours. This is especially important when collaborating with colleagues and contacts in different time zones. Tap Notifications and Quiet hours, and choose between which times your phone should be quiet from Teams notifications and also which days it applies to, as seen in Figure 3-6.

Another good feature of the mobile app is the setting to not receive notifications on your phone when you are active in Teams on your computer at the same time. This way, you avoid unnecessary notifications on your phone that you've already seen in your regular Team client.

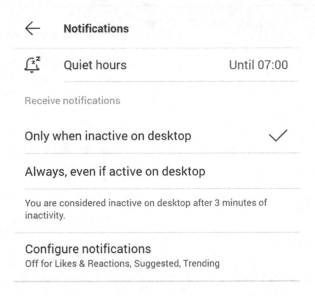

Figure 3-6. *Quiet hours in Teams mobile app*

Channel Conversations

Channel conversations occur within team channels. They provide a place where team members can discuss topics and post messages in which everyone in the team can reply.

One of the biggest benefits of channel conversations is a reduction in email and meetings through allowing teams to quickly reach decision points and discuss issues and tasks related to projects in real-time communication. Channel conversations differ from traditional email in that they are all in one viewable area for all team members. Email messages are stored within individual mail inboxes, which limits visibility for team members. Oftentimes, someone sends out an email about a topic to a group of people.

Then, that email is replied to without including the entire group, or forwarded to an individual, and the group context is lost. This results in team members being excluded from the series of emails and being left in the dark about key decisions and discussions related to the topic. And if you add an editable document to the email, it quickly gets even worse as you can imagine.

One of the key values in using channel conversations is that it preserves your organizational assets. In conversations, important information can be passed and decisions made between team members. If all the team members leave the organization, the information remains in the channel, in context, for you and others to view at a later time. When a new member joins the organization, department, or project, they are able to get up to speed. Having conversations stored in Microsoft Teams allows them to go to one place to read through conversations and quickly get up to speed.

To start a conversation

1. Navigate to the Posts tab of the channel of choice.

2. At the bottom of the Conversations tab, use the text box to type your message, and then click the arrow located on the bottom right of the text box.

Note   It is easy to accidentally start a new conversation instead of replying to an existing one, so pay extra attention when replying, as seen in Figure 3-7.

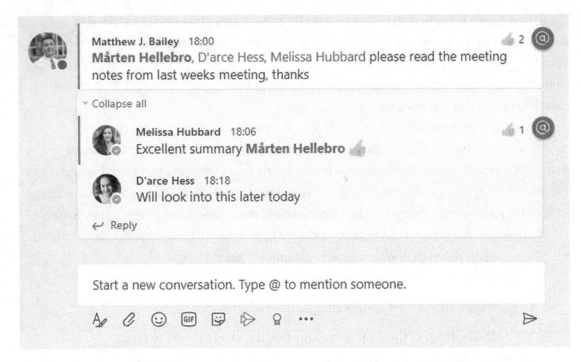

Figure 3-7. *Use **Reply** when replying and **Start a new conversation** when starting a new conversation*

Mentioning a Team Member, Channel, or Team

If you type the @ symbol followed by a team member's name, a channel name, or a team name (often referred to as at-mention, or @mention), a list of names that start with the few letters you type will show up for you to choose from. If you choose a person, they will receive a notification of the mention. If you choose a channel, everyone in the team receives a notification with the name of the channel being mentioned. If you choose a team, everyone who is part of the team receives a notification. This is a way to let a team member, channel, or team know that a message is directed to them and that they need to pay attention.

You can also mention a chatbot to get help answering questions or process certain things.

Note   The ability to @mention a team is a setting that the team owner controls and can therefor differ between different teams.

Liking a Message

One way to acknowledge that you have read someone's message and that you agree with them is to hit the Like button on their message. This is similar to Facebook's well-known Like functionality. The person who originally posted the message is notified that you liked it. You can unlike a message by clicking the same button again.

There are a couple of other ways to react to a message, use them with common sense to liven up, and keep conversations flowing and productive. From personal experience, I know that the heart does not mean that the person loves you.

To like or react to messages

1. Hover your mouse over the right corner of the message.

2. Click any of the reaction types that appears (see Figure 3-8).

Figure 3-8. *Reacting to a message*

Saving a Conversation Message

Conversation and chat messages can be saved to be read later. This is especially good if you have several messages that you need to follow up at a later time.

To save messages

1. Hover your mouse over the right corner of the message.

2. Select the three dots (More options).

3. Click **Save** this message, (see Figure 3-9).

Figure 3-9. *Saving a message*

To view saved messages

1. Click your picture icon in the top-right corner of the Microsoft Teams app.

2. Click **Saved**, as seen in Figure 3-10.

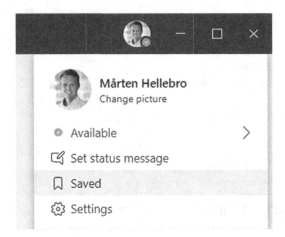

Figure 3-10. *Viewing all saved messages*

Message Formatting Options

Expanding the compose box shows more options for the message text. To expand the compose box, click the symbol with the letter A and a paint brush below the text box, as seen in Figure 3-11.

Figure 3-11. Additional message formatting options

When you do this, the functions to change the text font, size, and color will appear, as well as paragraph-formatting options, such as headings and bullets. The function to add a hyperlink is also found when you expand the compose box.

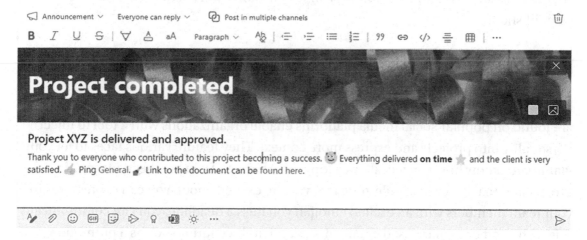

Figure 3-12. Example of when additional message formatting has been used

Note   A good rule is to use a Subject when you start a new conversation, in the same way as the subject of an email. It makes it easier to find, and everyone quickly sees what it's all about.

Additional Conversation Options

In addition to writing well-formulated and engaging messages, one can choose to create an announcement. It is a message type that stands out a little extra by adding a background image and an extra-large headline. Perfect when you want to catch everyone's attention with an extra good news, or the upcoming Christmas or summer party. Select Announcement found by clicking the New Conversation drop-down option, as seen in Figure 3-12.

Some messages can be more of a form of news or information where you may not want everyone to be able to reply. For these types of messages, you can choose to limit who can reply to only the person who wrote the post and those who are appointed as moderators for the channel; select You, and moderators can reply by clicking the Everyone can reply drop-down option, as seen in Figure 3-11.

Same message in multiple channels? Sometimes, the same message may need to be posted in several different channels; this is possible by selecting the Post in multiple channels as seen in Figure 3-11. Choose in which teams and channels the message will be published.

Using Emojis

Emojis allow team members to express emotions in chats and conversations. Emojis that are found on popular social media platforms enable organizations with a tool to inject personality into projects and express more context. They feature various faces to let your teammates know how you feel about a topic or message. If you are the manager of a project and reach a project milestone that you are excited about, you can express this to your team members with an excited emoji. If you miss a deadline, you can communicate this with a sad or embarrassed emoji. In work-related scenarios such as a promotion party for a team member or planning a happy hour event, emojis enable personality-based communication to add additional feeling to a project or task being managed in Microsoft Teams. If you don't know what a particular emoji means, you can place your cursor over the emoji to see its meaning, or you can use the search box. Emojis really let a person's personality be reflected within their words.

To add an emoji to a chat or conversation message

1.   Click the smiley face icon below the text box when adding a new chat or conversation message.

2. Either scroll through the emoji faces or use the search box to find an emotion, as seen in Figure 3-13.

Figure 3-13. *Adding emojis to a message*

GIFs

GIF is a type of file format that supports animated images. The animation contributes to a more vivid conversation without using a lot of words, perfect for those who struggle with the language or spelling, or simply don't have the time. And it is true what says, a picture says more than a thousand words, almost. Microsoft Teams comes with many GIFs that can be used in chat and conversation messages.

To add a GIF to a chat or conversation message

1. Click the GIF icon below the text box when adding a new chat or conversation message.

2. Either scroll through the GIFs or use the search box, as seen in Figure 3-14.

3. Select the GIF of choice.

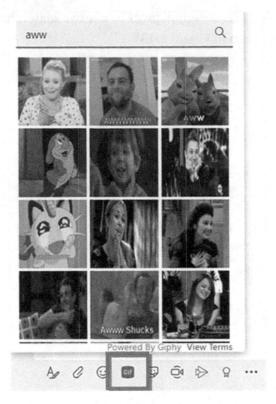

Figure 3-14. *Adding GIFs to a message*

Stickers

Stickers are editable images that can be sent in chat and conversation messages. Microsoft Teams comes with a wide variety of sticker templates. Stickers are a great way to have fun with your team. Microsoft Teams comes with images that you can edit with text to express emotions with a picture and customized message.

To add a sticker to a chat or conversation message

1. Click the square smiley sticker icon below the text box when adding a new chat or conversation message, as seen in Figure 3-15.

2. Either scroll through the stickers or use the search box.

3. Enter any desired text, and then click the **Done** button.

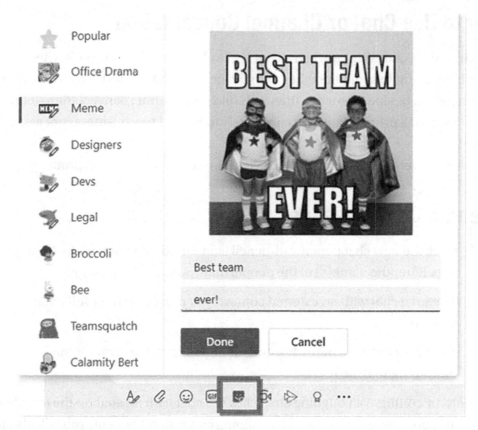

Figure 3-15. *Adding stickers to a message*

Chat

Chat in Microsoft Teams provides a way to have a 1:1 or group conversation and is great for those private or ad hoc conversations that do not belong in a channel conversation. The chat history is kept and made available on all your Teams devices. Continue yesterday's chat with a colleague or an external contact on your mobile while on the move today. Microsoft Teams offers chat capability with users within as well as outside of your organization, regardless if they are using Microsoft Teams or Skype for Business.

Note   Teams or Skype contacts outside of your organization can only be in a 1:1 chat, not a group chat. This might change in the future.

When to Use Chat or Channel Conversation

A good rule when choosing between a chat and a channel conversation is whether this may be relevant to someone other than the people who are currently in the chat, or if it concerns a business process, then it should be a channel conversation. If the conversation is of a private nature or completely unrelated to a business process, a chat is preferable.

Keeping conversations in channels makes it more transparent and productive.

To Send a Chat Message

- Click the new chat paper-and-pencil icon found in the top of the Chat app. Enter the name(s) of the people that you want to message.

- To start a chat with an external contact, you must type their full email address.

- Type your message in the text box, and then click the arrow at the bottom right of the text box.

To reply, or continue an ongoing chat, click the chat icon located on the left ribbon in the Teams app, where you will find all ongoing chats under Recent. You will also find missed chat messages under the Activity feed.

Manage Chats

There are several ways to organize your chats in Microsoft Teams. As mentioned earlier, all ongoing chats are listed under Recent, and this is an excellent view to keep track of all ongoing chats. By right-clicking your favorite chats, you can select to "pin" them so that they are always available at the top of the Recent list.

You can also name chats to further improve visibility. Select the down arrow found to the far right when initiating a new chat. For an existing chat, select the pencil icon found right next to the names of the participants at the top of the chat window, and type a descriptive name.

To increase productivity when you work in Microsoft Teams, you can choose to have one or more chats as separate windows, so you don't have to switch between different conversations inside Teams. Simply right-click, and select Pop out chat, or select the pop-out icon, as seen in Figure 3-16.

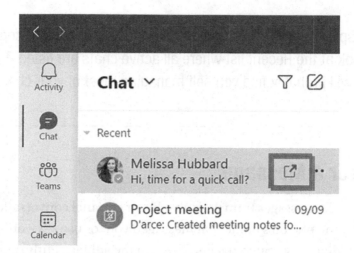

Figure 3-16. *"Popping out" a chat in a separate window*

You can easily add more participants to an ongoing chat by clicking the icon in the upper right corner that represents the number of participants in the chat. If you are already three or more participants, you'll get the choice to include chat history or not, and if so, how far back.

It's just as easy to remove attendees, click the icon in the upper right, and select the x after the name of the participant you want to remove from the chat.

Chat Contacts

If you're used to using Skype for Business, you'll quickly notice that Microsoft Teams handles contacts a little differently. One big difference is that your personal contacts in Outlook aren't searchable from Microsoft Teams. It also cannot add distribution lists from Outlook as contact groups in Teams. Of course, you can add your own contacts and create your own groups directly in Teams, and here's how to do this.

The easiest way to add a contact is to right-click a contact from an active chat and select Add to favorite contacts. This will add the contact to the Favorites group.

To add a contact to another group, first, create the group by selecting the Create a new contact group found at the bottom left-hand side, give the contact group a suitable name, and click create. Then click the three dots (...) next to the newly created group name, and select Add a contact to this group. Users within the organization are easily found by typing their name; to add an external contact, you need to enter the entire email address. Ignore the text saying We couldn't find any matches. Press enter, and select Search... Then click Add.

Note   Before spending too much time adding and arranging your contacts in contact lists, look at the Recent list where all active chats are listed. This is a great place, and you will probably find yourself managing most of your chats directly from here.

Searching for a Message

You can search for old messages from your chat list or channel conversations. Use the search bar to enter the person's name that messaged you, or use keywords from the message. You can filter your search results based on the subject, author, and date of the message.

Voice Calls

Sometimes, there is no time to type a chat message to a team member, or the context of the communication requires speaking. Teams to Teams or Teams to Skype voice calls are perfect for this situation. If you have ever used Skype for Business in the workplace, you will find the functionality very similar. You can voice call anyone within or outside your organization that is also using Teams or Skype, even if they are not a member of any of your teams.

Sharing your screen is another excellent feature when you want to collaborate with a teammate and typing a message is just not good enough. A screen sharing is initiated the same way as a call.

Note   In order to call external contacts outside your organization who also use Teams or Skype for Business, both organizations must allow external communication. Consumer Skype may have different settings as IT administrator can choose to manage these services differently. It is also possible to allow to alternatively block specific organizations from communicating.

To make a voice call

1. Click the chat icon located on the left in the Microsoft Teams app.

2. Either select the person you want to call from your recent list or use the search box to find them. You can create a new chat to make the call by following the previous instructions.

3. Click the phone icon located on the top right of the chat message, as seen in Figure 3-17. You will then be brought to the call screen as seen in Figure 3-18.

4. The person is notified with a ringing that they are receiving a Teams call. If they answer, the call begins; if not, they are notified that they have a missed call.

5. To share your screen, click the Share screen icon. A screen sharing can be set up whether you have a call running or not.

6. For more options, select the More actions (...) menu where you will find options for transfer, hold, start recording, and more.

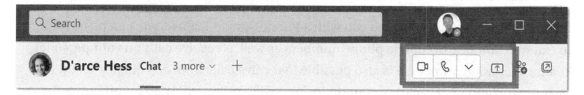

Figure 3-17. *Making a video or voice call, or share your screen*

Figure 3-18. *Calling a team member*

Phone Calls

If your organization has enabled you with a Phone System license, you can place calls to external landline or mobile phone numbers as well as receive calls on your personal Teams telephone number. It is also possible to receive calls from call queues set up by your organization if it is part of your duties. You will notice a dial pad found under the Calls app together with Call contacts and Speed dial contacts.

Along with your Teams phone number, there's also a personal voicemail where people can leave messages. You can listen to your voicemails in Teams by selecting the Voicemail option, as seen in Figure 3-19, or via the email that is also sent to your inbox.

Teams is a very competent phone system with numerous calling features available together with options to interact with other calling services. Which features and how you best utilize them is individual to all organizations; for the calling features available to you, please contact your IT admin for more information.

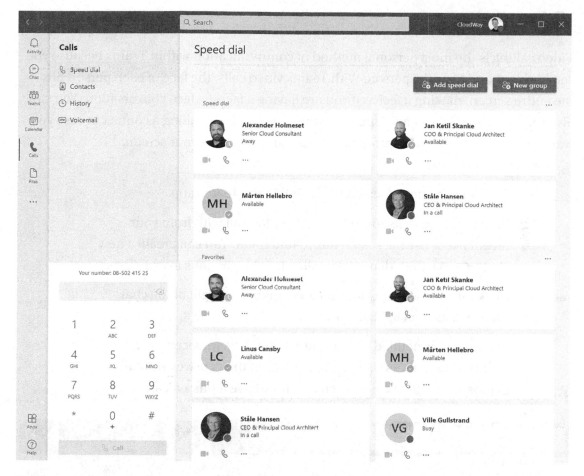

Figure 3-19. *Dial pad found under Calls when Phone System license enabled*

Call Settings

Common to both voice calls and phone calls is that you can decide how you want to manage your calls. Under **Settings** and **Calls** found by selecting your profile picture in the top right-hand corner in Teams, you'll find settings for how incoming calls should be handled and what should happen when you're not answering or being unavailable.

Video Calls

Video calling is the most personal method of communication within Teams because you can both see and hear the person. With Teams video calls, the face of each person fills the entire screen, making it feel as if you are having a face-to-face conversation. You can also send chat messages and share your screen while video calling a contact in case you want to send a link to a work product or share something on your screen.

To make a video call

1. Click the chat icon located on the left in the Teams app.

2. Either select the person you want to video call with from your recent list or use the search box to find them. You can create a new chat to make the video call by following the previous instructions.

3. Click the video camera icon located on the top right of the chat message, as seen in Figure 3-20.

4. The person is notified with a ringing that they are receiving a Teams video call, as seen in Figure 3-21. If they answer, the call begins; if not, they are notified that they have a missed call.

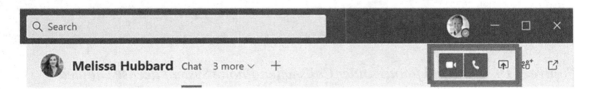

Figure 3-20. *Making a video call*

Answering Incoming Call

To answer an incoming call, click anywhere in the incoming call dialog, aka "toaster" popping up. You don't need to aim specifically at an icon, clicking anywhere in the dialog results in you accepting the call using audio only. To answer with your video on, you can select the video icon, or if you don't want to answer, select the red decline icon to send the call to voicemail, or any other option you selected for the not answering option.

Figure 3-21. Incoming call "toaster" from a team member

Audio Quality Matters

When you make voice calls, whether it's with one or more people, it's important that what you say clearly reach the recipient. Among the most annoying things during a call or meeting is bad audio; it can really kill off all creativity and efficiency. You probably recognize yourself in calls you have had with others when disturbing background noise, echo, or poor audio quality has made the conversation an unpleasant experience. The best way to avoid this is to use audio devices that are certified and optimized for Microsoft Teams; devices certified for Skype for Business work just as well. There are a whole plethora of different audio devices such as headsets and speakerphones from many different manufacturers and price ranges. Common to all certified Teams (and Skype) devices is that they are tested and meet all the basic requirements for good audio quality and compatibility, to ensure a good experience both for yourself and those you talk to.

So, put away the headphones that came with your mobile phone, and avoid as far as possible using the built-in speakers and microphone in your mobile or laptop.

Whether it's your employer providing devices, or you are purchasing them yourself, make sure they're Teams (or Skype) certified.

Choosing the Right Form of Communication

Microsoft Teams is a virtual workplace that addresses many forms of office communication. The channel conversations, the heart of Teams, this is where the real collaboration takes place. All team members collaborate on what is relevant right now, all the time in the right context, making it transparent and easy to follow along. Mixing text, emojis, announcements, GIFs, documents, likes, and hearts makes conversations more vivid and engaging.

You can have one-on-one communication with a team member by using chat. The topics discussed via chat are similar to discussions one would have when stopping by a team member's office or running into them in the break area. They are informal and usually have quick response times. You can see when your team members are available, away, or offline based on the color circle on the bottom right of their profile picture. Green means available, yellow is away, red means busy, and no color means they are offline.

Group chat is similar; it is for ad hoc discussions with a group of teammates. Group chat is one way to effectively reduce the need for formal meetings, which can be a waste of time. With group chats, you can convey a message quickly to multiple team members. You can also utilize audio and video calling to see and hear your teammates, which makes it more personal. If you want to post a message that all team members can reply to on their own schedule, you should utilize channel conversations. This is where work gets done.

Summary

In this chapter, we explored the many options in which you can communicate with other Microsoft Teams users. We discussed how to create conversations, start voice and video calls, add emojis and images, and how to chat. Choosing the right form of communication in Microsoft Teams is important to make sure that you're conveying your messages and ideas in the best manner. We also discussed how and why it is so important to manage your own Teams notifications. Now, let's move on to the different methods of meeting with others using Microsoft Teams.

CHAPTER 4

Meetings in Teams

There has been a lot of discussion and research in the business world over the last several years about the time, money, and resources wasted on meetings. Group chat and conversations in Microsoft Teams offer practical ways to discuss topics and make decisions without taking an hour or more out of several team members' day to be in a meeting together. There are situations, however, in which meetings are necessary. Whether you are in a meeting to discuss status updates, do a project code review, refine a sales plan, or for any other business reason, Microsoft Teams has a way to bring you together effectively and efficiently. Microsoft Teams has smart features that not only help you stay focused before, during, and after meetings but also reduce the time spent in meetings so your teams save time and accomplish more together. All with a consistent experience across devices, screen sizes, and platforms at home, in the office, in the conference room, or on the go.

There are a total of five different meeting experiences within Microsoft Teams: private meetings, channel meetings, ad hoc meetings, breakout room meetings, and live events. Not only does Microsoft Teams offer different meeting experiences, but there are also a few different ways to both schedule and join meetings. A plethora of meeting features allow for a smooth and customizable experience. Video, voice, screen sharing, and chat within the meeting offer a wide range of choices for communication style. In this chapter, we discuss the meeting options in Microsoft Teams as well as how to schedule, join, and participate in them.

Private Meetings

The first type of meeting that we discuss is the most traditional in that it resembles an Outlook meeting invitation, which is widely used. They can be between two individuals, or many people. Meetings can be scheduled directly through the Microsoft Teams app or through Outlook using an add-in. If you have Microsoft Teams and Microsoft Office installed on your device, the add-in shows up in Outlook automatically.

© Melissa Hubbard, Matthew J. Bailey, D'arce Hess, Mårten Hellebro 2021
M. Hubbard et al., *Mastering Microsoft Teams*, https://doi.org/10.1007/978-1-4842-6898-8_4

Formal vs. Informal Meetings

Before scheduling a meeting, you should ask yourself: What kind of meeting is this; is it a formal or informal meeting? Technically, they are the same and are scheduled the same way but with the difference that a formal meeting typically requires some kind of preparation. It usually involves a larger group of participants, an agenda, meeting notes, and generally less room for hiccups, compared to an informal meeting that barely requires any preparations or structure at all.

An agenda can be included in the meeting invite or added to the Meeting Notes found in the Teams meeting. Here, you can also add pre-reads, documents, whiteboard, and take meeting notes before, during, and after the meeting (seen in Figure 4-1).

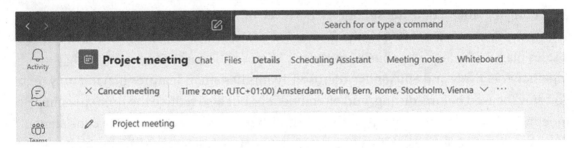

Figure 4-1. *Files, meeting notes, and whiteboard can be added to a Teams meeting beforehand*

Another important part of a formal meeting is to assign different meeting roles. Who should present and possibly share content during the meeting is fundamental, but also who should manage the virtual lobby (see Figures 4-19 and 4-20), moderate the meeting chat, and help mute anyone who accidentally disturbs the meeting (see Figure 4-21). All these roles are important to agree on before the meeting starts.

Scheduling Private Meetings

To schedule a meeting through the Microsoft Teams app

1. Click the **Calendar** icon located on the left-hand side in the Microsoft Teams app.

2. Click the **New meeting** button, as seen in Figure 4-2.

3. Fill out the title, start date and time, and end date and time, at a minimum, as seen in Figure 4-3.

4. In the **Add required attendees** field, select at least one person. Begin typing their name in the field, and then select them from the drop-down menu. You can add distribution lists as well as Office 365 Groups.

5. If you are inviting **someone outside of your organization**, you need to type in their **full email address** and select **invite** from the drop-down menu.

6. Click the **Send** button.

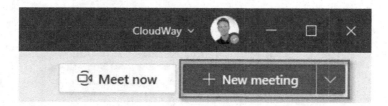

Figure 4-2. *Create a new Microsoft Teams meeting*

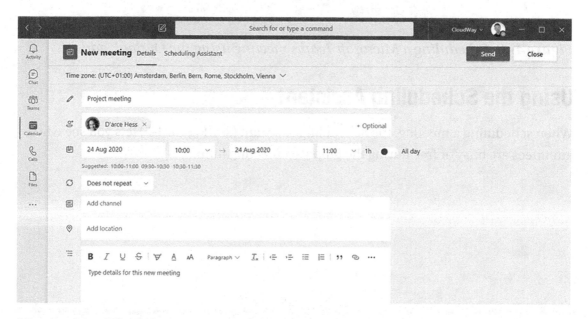

Figure 4-3. *Scheduling a Microsoft Teams meeting*

To schedule a meeting through the Outlook add-in

1. In the Outlook calendar, click the **New Teams Meeting** icon from
    the top ribbon, as seen in Figure 4-4.

2. Enter the meeting subject, start time, end time, and invitees.

3. Click the **Send** button.

Everyone invited will receive an email containing a link to join the meeting in Teams.

When using the Outlook add-in to schedule a Microsoft Teams meeting, you can
also click New Meeting, and then select Teams Meeting. This is just a different path to
get to the same destination in scheduling your meeting. From here, you can also start
an instant or an ad hoc meeting without sending out an invitation by selecting the Meet
Now feature.

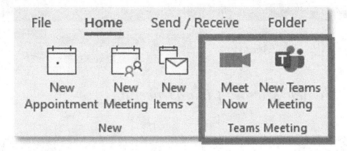

Figure 4-4. *Scheduling a Microsoft Teams meeting using the Outlook add-in*

Using the Scheduling Assistant

When scheduling a meeting, the Scheduling Assistant (see Figure 4-5) lets you see when
attendees are busy or free during the proposed meeting time.

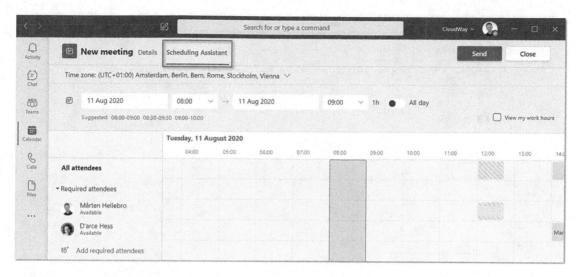

Figure 4-5. *Using the Scheduling Assistant in Microsoft Teams*

To use the Scheduling Assistant

1. Click the **Scheduling Assistant** link in the top ribbon.

2. Decide when to hold the meeting based on the attendee's availability.

3. Click **Send** or **Update**, depending on if you are creating a new meeting or updating an existing one.

Meeting Options

Each meeting has a set of meeting options, options like who (if any) should wait in the virtual lobby and who can present. The default settings are managed by your IT department, but you as a meeting organizer can set individual settings for each meeting. When you make these settings, keep security in mind so that privacy is not compromised depending on the type of meeting you are planning.

Access to the meeting options is available in the meeting invitation by clicking the **Meeting options** found at the bottom in both Outlook and Teams calendar (as seen in Figure 4-6). In Teams calendar, it might be necessary to first schedule and send out the meeting invitation before the meeting options become available.

Meeting options can also be found in the meeting itself, after you as a meeting organizer joins the meeting. Select **More actions** (...) and **Meeting options**.

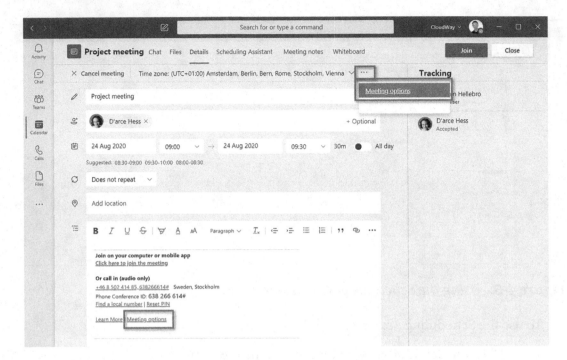

Figure 4-6. *Accessing the meeting options that sometimes is hiding under the tree dots (...)*

Make your selections accordingly (as can been seen in Figure 4-7), and keep in mind that these settings can be set and changed before, during, and after the meeting.

Meeting options

Who can bypass the lobby?	Everyone ∨
Always let callers bypass the lobby	Yes ●
Announce when callers join or leave	Yes ●
Who can present?	Everyone ∨
Allow attendees to unmute	Yes ●
Allow meeting chat	Enabled ∨
Allow reactions	Yes ●

Figure 4-7. *Meeting options selections*

For a highly confidential meeting, a good practice is to select that all participants should wait in the lobby by selecting **Only me** in the **Who can bypass the lobby** setting, and don't allow callers to bypass the lobby. This allows for you as the meeting organizer to control who is admitted into the meeting after being identified in the meeting lobby. The **Who can present** option is another security setting allowing you as a meeting organizer to control who can share content during the meeting but also manage the meeting lobby and other meeting organizer options. By setting it to **Only me**, you limit these privileges to only you, and when the meeting has started, you can allow individual participants the presenting privileges when required. Participants without the presenter role can participate in the meeting chat, share their video, and unmute themselves during the meeting.

Allow attendees to unmute is a setting that allows you as a meeting organizer to decide whether attendees should be able to unmute themselves during the meeting or not. It obviously depends on the type of meeting you are planning, and you as the meeting organizer can change this setting during the meeting for everyone through the Meeting options. With this setting set to **No**, you can instruct the participants to use the raise hand feature if they want to speak and then allow that participants to unmute themselves by making her or him a presenter (as seen in Figure 4-21).

From the meeting options, you can also decide if the meeting should have the meeting chat feature enabled or not, or if it should only be enabled during the meeting and then disabled after the meeting has ended. There is also an option to allow reactions during the meeting.

Inviting Unauthenticated Guests to Meetings

Teams provides a means to schedule a private meeting and invite someone that is completely outside of your organization and may not even have the Microsoft Teams app installed on their device (see Figure 4-8). The person just needs a valid email address to be invited to the private Microsoft Teams meeting and receive information on the meeting and how to join it. When clicking the join link, a browser page is opened asking the guest to either download the Teams desktop app or join on the Web instead.

The guest is prompted to enter their name when they click the link to join the meeting (although guests can also join anonymously), as seen in Figure 4-9. Guests that do not have the Microsoft Teams app can join using a web browser.

Note   While the Teams desktop app offers a richer meeting experience even for unauthenticated users, the web browser version is quicker and doesn't require any installation.

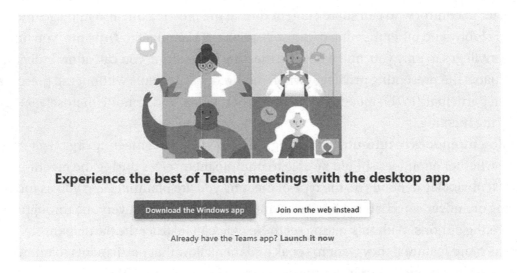

Figure 4-8. *Unauthenticated guest choosing between joining using Teams app and on the Web*

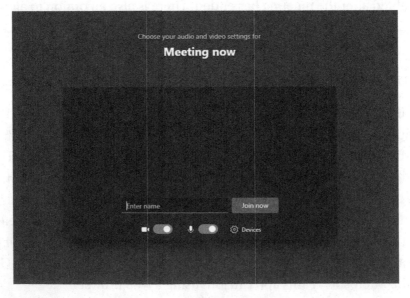

Figure 4-9. *Unauthenticated guest joining a meeting*

Holding virtual meetings with people from outside an organization is common. This meeting feature is useful when you need to have meetings with a client, stakeholder, contractor, vendor, or anyone that does not have an Office 365 account with your organization.

Joining Private Meetings

To join a meeting through the Teams desktop app

1. Click the **calendar icon** located to the left of the Teams app. All your upcoming meetings are shown in the calendar view.

2. Select the meeting that you wish to join, and click **Join. Or open the** meeting to see more information, and then click the Join button in the upper right-hand side of the meeting invite, or the **Click here to join the meeting** link located in the bottom of the meeting invite, as seen in Figure 4-10.

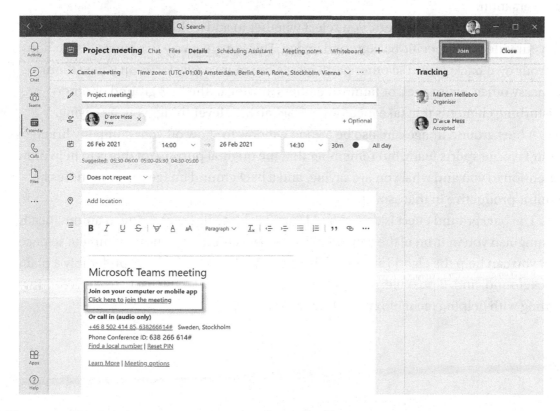

Figure 4-10. *Joining private meetings from the Teams app*

To join a meeting through the Outlook add-in

1. In the Outlook calendar, click the meeting to open the invite.

2. Click the **Click here to join the meeting link.**

The Pre-join Meeting Screen

Before entering the meeting, you are presented the pre-join meeting screen. Here, you can check your audio and video device settings prior to entering the meeting, like if you should have your video camera and microphone on or off and what audio device to use, among other things, as seen in Figure 4-11. Your selections from the previous meeting are remembered, so you probably won't need to change much from one meeting to the next.

If there are already several participants in the meeting, the pre-join screen will inform you about this and kindly suggest that you join the meeting with your microphone muted, so that you are not accidentally interrupting an ongoing conversation.

Under **Background filters**, you select whether to add a blurred background effect to your video or a specific background image. This is a great way to remove distractions in your own background so other participants can more easily focus on you without a messy office, colleagues, or family members moving in the background or other disturbing elements that take focus away from all the clever things you are saying.

A background image can also be a good window to show off your company brand or your favorite sports team, but remember that the original purpose of this is to help draw attention to you and what you are saying, and a background image can sometimes be contra-productive in that aspect.

The background effect is driven by AI (Artificial Intelligence) trying to automatically distinguish you in front of the camera from the background. It is not a complete science, but you can help the algorithms by assuring you have a good lighting, preferably a plain background, and, if possible, dress in contrasting colors from the background. Nothing wrong with helping technology a little along the way.

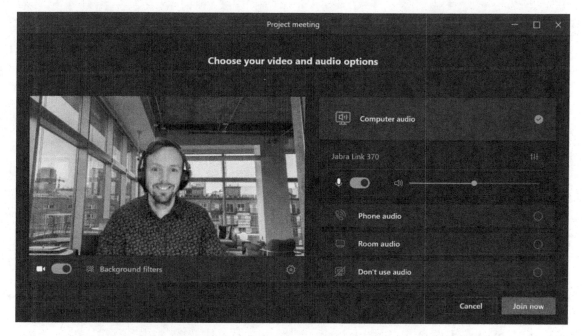

Figure 4-11. *Set your preferred setting before joining a meeting from the Teams app*

Channel Meetings

Channel meetings (see Figure 4-12) are scheduled meetings that occur in a channel within a team. Channel meetings offer many benefits. One benefit is that they make it possible to quickly invite everyone from a team to a meeting. Another benefit is that information about the meeting is saved in the channel as an organizational asset. While working in Teams, it is obvious to team members that a meeting is occurring in a channel: a camera icon appears to the right of the channel name. In the channel conversations, a large message is posted when the meeting starts. The message shows each person who has joined the meeting by displaying their profile pictures in a small circle in the top right of the message. At the bottom of the meeting message, you see the chat. Additionally, a timer shows how long the meeting has been taking place.

While a channel meeting is restricted to people already being a member of the team holding the channel where the meeting is hosted, it is possible to invite external contacts to a channel meeting. But the meeting experience will not be great because the external contacts will not have access to all features and assets of the meeting like the team members do, for example, the meeting chat. So, when inviting external contacts to a meeting, the recommendation is to not use channel meetings.

Figure 4-12.   *Ongoing channel meeting*

Scheduling Channel Meetings

Channel meetings can only be scheduled through the Microsoft Teams app (not with the Outlook add-in). Team members won't receive an email notification when a channel meeting is scheduled; to inform team members of the meeting, add them to the required attendees filed in the meeting invite.

Note   After a meeting completes, the total time of the meeting, the meeting attendees, any attached files, and the chat are saved in the channel automatically.

To schedule a channel meeting

1. Click the **Calendar icon** located on the left in the Microsoft Teams app.

2. Click the **New meeting** button.

3. Fill out the title, start date and time, and end date and time, at a minimum.

4. Pick a channel from the **Add channel** drop-down menu, as seen in Figure 4-13.

5. Click the **Send** button.

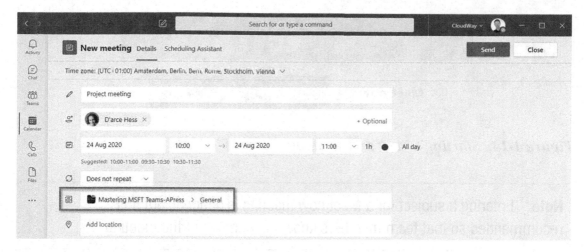

Figure 4-13. Scheduling a channel meeting

Meet Now Meetings

Meet now or ad hoc meetings allow spontaneous meetings with colleagues, guests, and external contacts. Since no one is invited to a Meet now meeting, participants must be either added from within the meeting or sent the meeting join link manually. To add participants to the meeting, select **Participants** and search for a contact, or select **More actions** (…), **Meeting details**, and click **Copy join info**, and send that information to anyone that should participate in the meeting.

To start a Meet now meeting

1. Click the **Meet now** icon located next to the New meeting button at the top right-hand corner in the Calendar tab in Teams (see Figure 4-14).

2. Enter a subject for the meeting, and make any other preferred settings before clicking the **Join now** button.

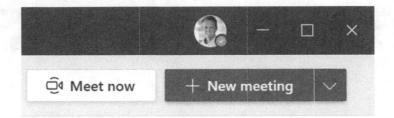

Figure 4-14. *Starting a Meet now meeting*

Note   Entering a subject for a Meet now meeting is optional, but it is recommended so that team members know the purpose of the meeting.

Breakout Rooms

Breakout rooms allow organizers to divide the meeting to facilitate discussions and brainstorming sessions in subgroups. The idea is that all participants are invited to a regular Teams meeting, acting as the "main" meeting. From here, the meeting organizer can assign participants into smaller groups to meet in separate breakout rooms. This can be done either by dividing participants automatically between the available breakout rooms or manually adding participants to specific rooms.

The breakout room structure is created by the meeting organizer joining the meeting preferably beforehand.

1. Select the **Breakout rooms** icon, as seen in Figure 4-15.

2. Select how many breakout rooms to create.

3. Select how to assign participants to the breakout rooms, automatically or manually.

4. Breakout rooms created.

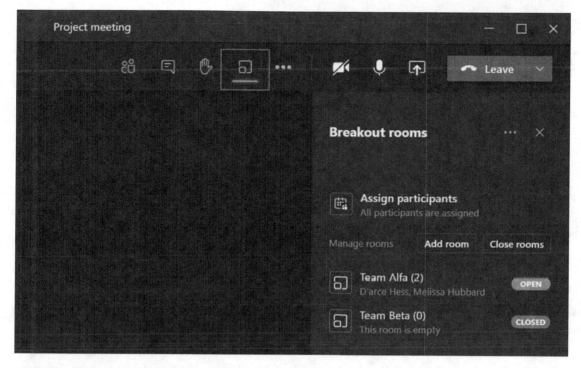

Figure 4-15. *Create breakout rooms*

The breakout rooms are now ready but still not activated. If you want, you can rename the rooms by right-clicking and selecting Rename room. This can truly help you, and the participants, keep track of the different rooms.

When participants have joined the main meeting and it is time to divide the group into smaller groups, the meeting organizer starts the rooms by selecting the Start rooms icon or individual rooms by right-clicking the room and selecting Open room. This will automatically transfer the assigned participants to the designated breakout room, and participants will see a message informing them that they will automatically be transferred to a breakout room.

A breakout room can only be started if it has at least one participant assigned to it. So, make sure you assign all participants to a room if you didn't choose to assign them automatically in the beginning. This is also true for any late joiners; they need to be manually assigned to a room.

As the meeting organizer, you can jump in and out of any breakout room and the main meeting. You can also make announcements with chat messages in all breakout rooms at the same time. This is a good feature to inform all participants that it is soon time to meet in the main meeting again, for example.

When the time is up, you can close the breakout room forcing participants to automatically rejoin the main meeting to report their conclusions or just summarize and end the meeting.

Note   In the backend, all breakout rooms are individual Teams meetings which means that all meeting features and settings are available, and all governance settings apply.

Joining a Meeting by Audio Conference

Participants in Microsoft Teams meetings can join meetings by phone while they are on the go. This is useful when a meeting participant does not have access to the Internet. For meeting organizers who have the feature enabled for them, the dial-in instructions are automatically added in the Teams meeting invite being sent to invitees.

The dial-in phone number shown in the invitation is controlled by the organizers' location; if you receive a meeting invitation and the phone number does not match your location, you can click on the link **Find a local number** and find a suitable number to avoid international calling fees, as seen in Figure 4-10.

Note   Only meeting organizers that have the Audio Conferencing license added by the Office 365 administrator have the dial-in instructions.

Meeting Controls for Participants

Participants in Microsoft Teams meetings have control over how they participate in a meeting and what they share. To get the most out of meetings, use of video and voice is recommended. However, participants can choose whether they show themselves in a video or use voice. Microsoft Teams has a feature that allows you to share your screen or choose which window on your desktop that you want to share, in case you don't want people to see your email or anything else that is personal. The controls for participants are available in the top row of the meeting window, as seen in Figure 4-16.

Figure 4-16. *Participant meeting controls*

Muting the Mic

When a participant has their mic open, and there is background noise, it can be very distracting for everyone in the meeting. It is best practice to keep the mic muted unless you are speaking. If you are speaking and no one is responding to you, check your mic because you may have forgotten to unmute yourself!

Click the **microphone icon** to mute yourself, as seen in Figure 4-16. To unmute, follow the same instructions. The microphone icon has a slash going through it when muted.

Disabling Video

Communicating with other meeting participants is best with video. When people can see your expressions along with hearing you speak, they are the most likely to understand your message. For the times that you do not want others to see you, such as when you aren't in a professional meeting mood or you are multitasking, video can easily be disabled.

To disable the video, click the **camera icon**, as seen in Figure 4-16. To turn the video back on, follow the same instructions. If your video is turned off, your profile picture will light up when you talk, so others can see that you are talking.

Screen Sharing

Screen sharing is an extremely valuable feature. Common uses of screen sharing are to show presentation slides or to walk participants through some process or work tool. Participants can share content using Teams app, Teams web, and Teams mobile app. You also have the option to include system audio if you are sharing a video clip or other media containing audio that you want the other participants to hear.

To share content

1. Click the computer screen/arrow icon, as seen in Figure 4-17.

2. Choose whether you want to share your desktop, an open window, a PowerPoint presentation, or start a Whiteboard session.

3. Tick the box **Include computer sound** to add audio.

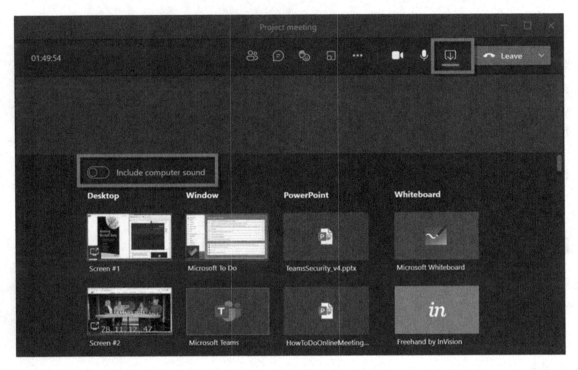

Figure 4-17. *Share content during a meeting*

To end content sharing, click the computer screen icon that now shows an "x."

Note   Sharing your desktop or a window using Teams on the Web is similar to sharing it from the desktop app but with the difference that you first have to select Desktop/Window, followed by specifying either desktop, a window, or a browser tab.

Giving Control of the Screen

When a presenter is sharing something, another participant may need to take control of their screen or application to demonstrate something. A participant can both give control of their screen and request control, as seen in Figure 4-18.

To give control of the screen

1. Click the **Give control** drop-down menu located on the top center of the screen currently being shared.

2. Select the person's name that you want to give control to.

3. From the drop-down menu, you can also include, or exclude, system audio from being shared, and stop the screen sharing.

Figure 4-18. Give control while screen sharing

Note   Giving control to others is a feature that must be allowed by your organization; if it isn't available to you, contact your IT administrator.

Meeting Reactions

React during a meeting using emojis that will appear to all participants. This is a great feature to show the presenter your instant feedback, without interrupting the meeting. Click the high-five icon (as seen in Figure 4-19), and select the appropriate reaction. This is also where you will find the raise your hand feature.

Raise Hand

Sometimes, it can be difficult to make yourself heard in a lively debate. Then the raise hand function is a good feature (as seen in Figure 4-19). Everyone in the meeting sees who has raised their hand, and the meeting organizer also sees the order in which people have raised their hands. Compared to raising your hand in real life, this is much gentler on your shoulder, but don't forget to lower your hand when you have lightened your heart.

Tip   This feature can also be used for answering questions with a raised hand and for voting. What else can it be used for? It's up to you and your teammates' creativity.

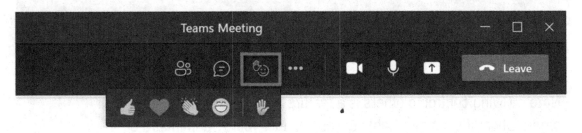

Figure 4-19. *Show some love or excitement during a meeting, or raise your hand to speak*

Polls

Polls in Teams meetings enable meeting organizers to get real-time feedback from participants and at the same time create a more engaging meeting. By selecting the Polls icon (as seen in Figure 4-20), you can create a new poll with questions for your meeting participants, select if it should allow multiple answers, if the results should be shared automatically, and whether to keep responses anonymous or not.

Polls are powered by Microsoft Forms, and if you don't see the Polls icon in the meeting, you need to add Forms as a tab to the meeting first. To add Forms as a tab to a Teams meeting, select the + sign found in the meeting entry in Microsoft Teams calendar, and select to add Forms.

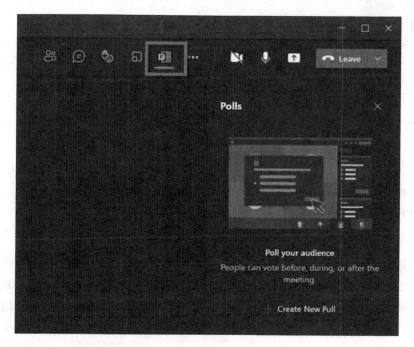

Figure 4-20. *Start a poll during a meeting*

More Actions

Under **More actions (…)**, you find a lot more features available to you as a meeting participant. In addition to switch audio and video devices and background settings that you've already seen in the pre-join meeting screen when you joined the meeting, you'll also find a lot of other features, like the option for different views. A view is how you see other meeting participants and shared content during the meeting, like how many participants are displayed at the same time. In the Together mode, everyone, including yourself, is placed in a scene where you get the feeling that you are all sitting together. If you haven't tried the Together mode, do it; chances are you'll like it! These settings apply only to how you see the other participants during the specific meeting; other participants can make their own view settings.

If you are authorized to record the meeting, this is where you start and stop the recording; the same applies to live captions that are also activated from here.

There are more options here, and with the utmost certainty, there will be even more meeting features added here in the future. A good idea is to regularly look through this menu to see if something new and exciting has been added since the last time.

Hanging Up a Meeting

To hang up a meeting

1. Click the **Leave** button.

2. This will disconnect you from the meeting without affecting the meeting itself, and it is possible to reconnect to the same meeting again.

3. Depending on what settings the meeting organizer has selected, you might still have access to the meeting chat.

Note   Hanging up a meeting does not mean the meeting will end, not even when the last participant leaves, or when you as the meeting organizer hangs up. The meeting will be idle, and it is possible to reconnect to the same meeting later on.

Meeting Controls for Organizers

Meeting organizers and presenters have additional controls in place that allow them to make sure the meeting runs smoothly. Organizers and presenters can admit participants into the meeting from the lobby, mute participants, start and stop recordings, remove participants, and more.

Record a Meeting

If you've been assigned recording rights, you can start and stop recording through the **More actions (...)** menu and **Start/Stop recording**. For regular Teams meetings, the recording is stored in the person who initiates the recording's OneDrive and the Recording folder. Shortly after the recording is stopped, a message appears in the meeting chat with information about the recording. Everyone that was part of the meeting has access to the recording.

Channel meeting recordings are stored in the teams SharePoint site and are available in the Files tab for the specific channel. This way, the recording is available to all members of the team, not just those who participated in the meeting.

Admitting Participants from the Lobby

One of the jobs of the meeting organizer, or a designated person with the presenter role, is to identify participants in the virtual meeting lobby and then admit authorized participants into the meeting. Depending on the subject matter of the meeting, it may be very important to carefully review the names of the participants waiting in the lobby. If something sensitive is being discussed, you do not want someone that should not be attending to get into the meeting.

To admit a participant from the lobby

1. Click **Admit** on the toaster seen in the meeting screen, as seen in Figure 4-21.

2. Or, click the **Green check mark** to the right of the participant's name, as seen in Figure 4-22.

3. Clicking the red X to the right of the person's name rejects the person from joining the meeting.

Figure 4-21. Admitting participants from the lobby in the meeting screen

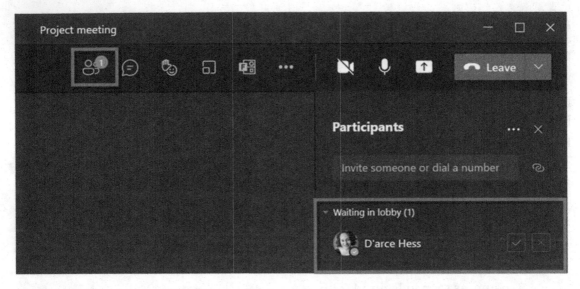

Figure 4-22. *Admitting participants from the lobby using the participant's pane*

Muting Participants

At times, a participant may not realize that they have their mic open, or they may have stepped away from their desk. If your meeting is being disrupted by background noise or someone having a conversation outside of the meeting, the organizer or a presenter can mute participants. You will know who is making the noise because the meeting tells you who is currently speaking. There is also an option to mute all participants; this is especially useful when there are a large number of participants in a meeting. This will mute all participants except yourself, so if anyone else is currently speaking, they will be muted.

To mute a participant

1. Right-click or select the ellipse (...) to the right of the participant's name in the list of participants currently in the meeting.

2. Click **Mute participant**, as seen in Figure 4-23.

The participant will be able to unmute their mic when they want to speak again and when the current distraction is fixed.

Note   Use the **Mute all** feature with extra care since it could potentially also mute the presenter currently speaking.

Figure 4-23. *Options available to meeting organizer and presenters during a meeting*

Pin and Spotlight

By selecting a participant to be on **Spotlight** (as seen in Figure 4-23), you select that person's video to be shown in full screen on all participants' screens; this is useful when you want to highlight a specific person during his or her speech or similar. Meeting organizers and presenters have this option.

With the **Pin** option (also as seen in Figure 4-23), you decide for yourself whose video you want to see on your screen, much like a personal spotlight feature which does not affect how other participants experience the meeting. This is available to all participants, and you can pin one or more participants' video. To unpin, simply select **Unpin**.

The Presenter and Attendee Roles

In a formal meeting with multiple participants, it is a good practice to assign roles to different participant to decide who should do what in the meeting. There are currently two roles: presenter and attendee. **Presenters** can as the name indicates present but also do just about anything that needs to be done during a meeting, while the **Attendee** role is limited to speak, share video, and participate in the meeting chat.

As the meeting organizer, you can choose who should join as a presenter; others will join as attendees. This is set in the Meeting options found in the meeting invitation but can also be found in the meeting itself by clicking More actions (…) and selecting Meeting options.

To promote an attendee to a presenter during the meeting

1. Right-click or select the ellipse (…) to the right of the participant's name in the list of people currently in the meeting.

2. Select **Make a presenter**, as seen in Figure 4-23.

3. To demote a presenter to an attendee, follow the same procedure.

Removing Participants

At times, a participant may be too disruptive or is invited in error. In these situations, the meeting organizer can remove a participant.

To remove a participant

1. Right-click or select the ellipse (…) to the right of the participant's name in the list of people currently in the meeting.

2. Select **Remove from meeting**, as seen in Figure 4-23.

3. This will remove the participant from the meeting, and if the participant is an external contact, he or she will also be removed from the meeting chat. Removing a participant will however not prevent the user from rejoining the meeting.

Meeting Chat

Each meeting has its own meeting chat where participants can chat; you'll find the meeting chat not only in the meeting itself but also among your regular chats in Teams. As a meeting organizer, you have a few different choices for how the meeting chat should behave before, during, and after the meeting. Depending on the type of meeting, it may be important to be in control of the chat so that sensitive information is not shared with unauthorized people by closing the chat after the meeting has ended or by removing participants who should no longer be part of the chat. Currently, there is no possibility to delete the chat history.

Meeting Attendance Report

Meeting organizers can download a meeting attendance report from the current meeting. The report is found in the Participants pane and contains information about participants, time joining and leaving the meeting. This can be useful when you as a meeting organizer wants to know who joined the meeting and stayed for how long.

Note   This feature must be enabled by an IT administrator and may be subject to compliance concerns.

End a Meeting

When the meeting is over, you as the meeting organizer might want to end the meeting by selecting **End meeting**, as shown in Figure 4-24. It will remove all participants from the meeting, but it will not delete the meeting; the meeting will remain, and it is possible to rejoin the meeting and continue the meeting chat.

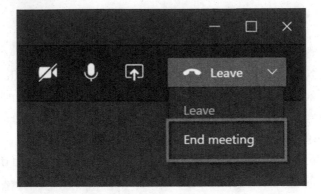

Figure 4-24. *A meeting organizer ends a meeting*

Teams Live Events

When you want to reach a larger audience than what a Teams meeting can offer, there's a feature called Teams live events that can help you with that. It differs in some respects compared to a "normal" Teams meeting. In a Teams live event, there are a limited number of presenters, but they have the potential to present for tens of thousands of attendees. Attendees can enjoy presentations, audio and video in the event, but not talk or share content themselves. The attendees can communicate through a question and answer chat module where they can write questions to a moderator. The moderator can reply, either privately or publicly, so all attendees can see the question and answer.

To produce a Teams live event requires some preparation; first, you choose your stellar team of live event members. Depending on how advanced you want to do your live event, the number of people in your event group can differ. But generally, there must always be at least one, but preferably two producers; it is they who control the broadcast. Then you need someone to present in the meeting; and it is also good to have a designated Q&A moderator. Technically, all producers and presenters have the Q&A moderator role, but to make it clear of who is in charge, it is a good practice to delegate the main responsibility to someone. The Q&A moderator keeps track of incoming questions, typing replies, and forwards questions to the presenter when needed. These roles are defined when you schedule the live event, which you do in your Teams calendar, as can be seen in Figure 4-25.

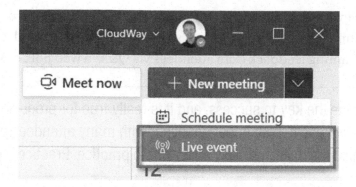

Figure 4-25. *Create a new Teams live event*

Create a Teams Live Event

In addition to appoint your event group and assigned desired roles, you need to decide who can watch the event. You have the option to allow specific people or groups in your organization as attendees, or to make it open to everyone within your organization. You can also make it public so that anyone can watch.

Whether the event should be recorded or not is also something you need to decide while scheduling the live event, and whether the recording should be made available to the event group only or also to the attendees. You also choose if you are to use the Q&A module or not.

Now you've created a Teams live event! Everyone in the event group receives a Teams meeting invitation that they use to join the event as a presenter or producer, when the time has come. Attendees have a separate attendee link that you need to distribute to them separately, which you can see in Figure 4-26.

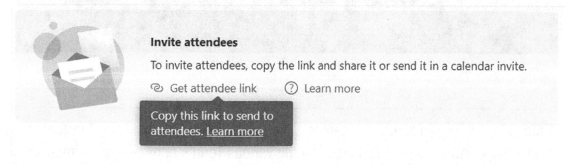

Figure 4-26. *Invite attendees by sending them the attendee link*

A Teams live event has a buffering delay of about 20–30 seconds, to compensate for poor network connections and such. That is something to keep in mind when you are presenting and wanting feedback from attendees via Q&A, a web poll, or similar.

Note   Practice is the key to success, and it is really true for producing a live event. Often, a live event is an important event with many attendees and without room for any hiccups; therefore, it is important to practice. Practice a lot.

The presenter of a live event uses the Teams desktop app to present, and it works very much like presenting in a regular Team meeting. However, the producer, who also uses the Teams desktop app, has a completely different view, as seen in Figure 4-27. The producer starts and stops the broadcast, choosing between the presenter's video and content sharing, or a combination of the two, to be broadcast live.

Figure 4-27. *Teams live event producer view*

Note   Currently, producers, presenters, and Q&A moderators must use the Teams desktop app. Attendees can connect via the various Teams apps and anonymously via a web browser.

When the live event is finished, the producer selects to end the broadcast. This will end the broadcast, and there is no option to continue or restart the live event after that. If the option to make recording available to attendees was selected, attendees will be able to connect to the live event even after the broadcast was ended to watch the recorded content, much like an on-demand video stream.

Note   Teams live events are included in most Microsoft 365 license packages, but not all, so make sure you have the correct license before you plan to start using live events.

Teams in the Conference Room

Meetings happen everywhere, at home, in the office, in a conference or meeting room, and on the go. And with Microsoft Teams consistent experience across devices, you would expect to conduct a Teams meeting in a conference or meeting room just as easy as from your own desk. And you can, with the right equipment.

Microsoft Teams Room (often referred to as MTR) is a collection of purpose-built meeting solution equipment from a broad set of third-party manufacturers with native Teams experience. It offers the most comprehensive set of Teams meeting features in a shared conference room in different sizes. It pairs with certified A/V peripherals, and it can also join Skype for Business meetings as well as Cisco and Zoom meetings.

In a conference room equipped with a Microsoft Teams Room system, you will find one or two monitors in front of the room and a meeting control panel on the table. From the control panel, you have full control over the meeting, so you can focus on what's being said and shared during the meeting while enjoying the most comprehensive set of Teams meetings and callings features available.

Collaboration bars are purpose-built meeting and calling solutions for smaller meeting rooms, sometimes referred to as huddle rooms, where you normally don't expect to have a HD audio and video conferencing equipment available. Compared to Microsoft Teams Room systems, collaboration bars are smaller and more compact and often combined in a single unit. If you connect it to a touch screen, you have a complete meeting system (you can also control the device with a remote control). They do not offer the same rich flora of features but quite enough for most informal meetings in the small meeting rooms and with the well-known Teams experience. Collaboration bars are available from several third-party manufacturers.

Microsoft Surface Hub is an all-in-one meeting and co-creation solution optimized for touch and pen experience. It is best suited for focus and huddle rooms where you can get creative with the whiteboard, for example. The Surface Hub can also be extended to larger rooms and linked with a Microsoft Teams Room to take your and your teams' creativity to unexpected heights.

All these devices are booked using Outlook or Teams, and when the time has come for the meeting to start, you simply approach the device, and with a one-touch join experience, you have joined the Teams meeting and are up and running in no time, hassle-free.

Audio Quality Matters

As we discussed in the previous chapter on audio calls, the audio quality is crucial for a good and productive conversation, and it also applies to meetings. A Teams-certified headset is a requirement for a great meeting experience. So please, put away the headphones that came with your mobile phone and avoid as far as possible using the built-in speakers and microphone in your mobile or laptop, for everyone's sake.

Summary

In this chapter, we walked through the multiple ways to hold meetings in Teams, as well as the different meeting controls for meeting organizers, presenters, and participants. The meeting features in Teams are very helpful for driving productivity and reducing time spent in meetings especially for teams that are not able to hold meetings in person. When members of an organization realize the value of holding not more but more effective and efficient meetings using Microsoft Teams, it helps drive user adoption of the product. More about user adoption of Microsoft Teams is covered in the next chapter.

CHAPTER 5

User Adoption in Teams

Have you seen eyes rolling and heard the moaning when a memo is sent out telling you and your teammates of a new intranet that they will need to use? Have you felt annoyed when you are told by leadership that there is a change to the performance review process and system, which is the third change in two years? If you ask information technology leaders what the biggest challenges of implementing new software are, user adoption will be at the top of the list.

User adoption is when the members of an organization accept and use a new software or tool that has been introduced to their work environment to its fullest extent. Organizations struggle with this for a variety of reasons. People simply do not like to change their work habits once they are a rhythm, even if it will save them time and make their life easier in the long run. This is especially true when they have a high workload or stress at work. It is difficult to switch gears and use a new software or tool when organization members are struggling to meet deadlines or have conflicting priorities. Also, there is often a lack of trust in new software or tools. If an organization has suffered through failed rollouts of software in the past, end users become disenchanted when they hear of something new. This is especially true if many people lost work and/or time, or if this is the perception.

External circumstances can affect the attitude and ability to adopt new systems and working methods in a positive direction, as the Corona pandemic has clearly shown. But it's not something we can plan for or hope will happen. By having a thorough plan for user adoption, you have at the same time given yourself greater flexibility to adapt the plan to changing circumstances.

Note   User adoption planning is just as important as implementation planning, so do not cut corners. It will not matter how smoothly the technical implementation of Microsoft Teams goes if there is weak user adoption.

© Melissa Hubbard, Matthew J. Bailey, D'arce Hess, Mårten Hellebro 2021
M. Hubbard et al., *Mastering Microsoft Teams*, https://doi.org/10.1007/978-1-4842-6898-8_5

Training can also be an issue in user adoption. Well-intentioned organization members may try to adopt a new software or tool but struggle with how to use it properly. If they can't quickly resolve it, they are likely to go back to old tools or to find work-arounds that do not involve the new software.

Many IT professionals have watched these user adoption issues plague their collaboration software rollouts for years. Many lessons have been learned that can be drawn upon to ensure that organizations are successful with Microsoft Teams user adoption.

One important lesson, if not the most important lesson, is that a Teams project is NOT an IT project. Exactly what kind of project it is is difficult to say because it differs between different organizations, but in general, it is a change and work cultural project. IT must be involved, no question about it, but by treating the Teams rollout as an email server upgrade, the project is doomed to failure. Make sure that all parts of the business are involved and that those who are best at driving change are the ones who lead the project; often, it is HR.

When to Use What for Collaboration

Microsoft 365 contains a collection of tools for collaboration and by knowing which tool to use when significantly simplifies the user adoption process. Yammer is a Microsoft 365 tool for enterprise-wide social networking and sharing information. Another tool is Microsoft 365 Groups. Microsoft 365 Groups provide a shared workspace that includes email, conversations, files, and events in which members of a group can collaborate and get work completed. The important distinction to make here is that Microsoft Teams is a platform with even more features, although in some ways they are connected in the background and Teams stitches the different services together for a holistic approach on collaboration.

There are many reasons to use Microsoft Teams. Although a single team can have up to 20,000 members, we do not recommend using Microsoft Teams solely for sharing organizational-level announcements and information. Microsoft Teams is not meant to replace an organization's intranet; however, we are seeing more and more of this, and with Microsoft Viva, it is easier than ever to connect, share, and find all kinds of information and assets within the organization, all available in Teams.

Knowing when to use which tool can sometimes be a bit confusing. To help guide you a bit more, Figure 5-1 is based on Microsoft's "inner circle/outer circle" reference.

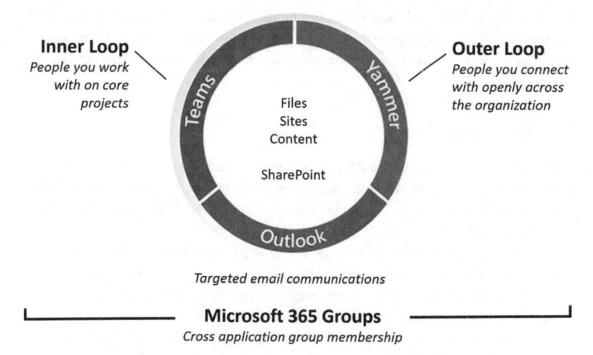

Figure 5-1. *Microsoft's recommendation of when to use which collaboration tool*

User Adoption Tips

User adoption is an art and a science. The most important thing is to have a strategy, but be flexible enough to make adjustments if something isn't working. Your organization may already have lessons learned about user adoption from previous software rollouts that can be drawn upon when rolling out Microsoft Teams. These tips are a great starting point. Another tip is to take the rollout in stages, starting with chat, calls, and meetings, for example. And when that has received broad acceptance, move on with team and channel conversations, files, tabs, and apps as an example.

Change Management

There are several different methods to manage the change process in a rollout project and to drive user adoption in a structured way. Common to these is that it starts with the individual, to envision and make them understand why this change is being made.

What's in it for me? It's also about enthusing, building knowledge and skills, and then continuing to build on it to make the change last and drive value over time. Commit to your organization's change management processes, and make sure you align with the right people.

Define Your Vision

The first step of having a successful Microsoft Teams implementation is deciding to use it for the right reasons. The key target business scenario for adopting Microsoft Teams is a group of team members working on the same job function or project that need to chat, collaborate, and hold meetings.

Additionally, before rolling out Microsoft Teams, it is a good idea to identify why you are rolling out Microsoft Teams in the first place. Although Microsoft Teams is new and exciting software, adding it because everyone else is, or because it is new, is not necessarily the best reason to deploy it. Understanding the challenges your users experience in the workplace and how Microsoft Teams can address those challenges helps with adoption. The following are some of the ways that Microsoft Teams can address these challenges:

- Makes remote users feel more connected, as though they are working in the same office

- Saves time by not having to open multiple applications to collaborate with other workers

- Save time, money, and the environment by not having to travel for meetings and remote location work all the time

- Improves the findability of related artifacts by having them in one location

Of course, each organization's reasoning is different, but taking the time to identify the reasons helps you create a foundation for a successful Microsoft Teams rollout.

Management Buy-in

Despite your or the IT department's best intentions, it is unlikely that it is sufficient to deliver a complete and successful rollout project in most organizations. You need to have the proper support from senior management. The idea is not to have them involved in the project itself but rather align with them and use them as extra weight and leverage justifying the change that are about or already being rolled out in the organization. Especially if things start to go sideways, then their support can be crucial in not losing momentum or acceptance. So, don't forget to keep the management up to date and happy.

Communicate the Benefits

It is common to draw an equal sign between communication and user training, but they are not the same. While training focusing on teaching users how to use a tool, communication campaigns focusing on the benefits to the users. Some organizations have staff members whose main role is to develop and carry out communication strategies. For other organizations, it is sufficient to bring up Microsoft Teams in meetings or to post an announcement on the intranet.

Identify the Right Team Owners

Team owners interface with team members, and it is important that the owners have a positive attitude and thorough understanding of how Microsoft Teams works. Team owners should feel empowered to make decisions and try new ways to use Microsoft Teams to maximize the benefits. Forcing someone who is too busy to be a team owner, or who is uninterested in being a team owner, is detrimental to user adoption.

Ways Team Owners Can Engage Team Members

The best way for team owners to engage their team members is to set a shining example of how Microsoft Teams should be used. When team owners notice a long group email conversation, they should respond, "Let's take this conversation to Microsoft Teams." Often, team members suggest holding a meeting to discuss something that could be handled in conversations in Microsoft Teams. Team owners can start a conversation in Microsoft Teams and let team members know that time could be saved if the subject is discussed there.

If a team member is slow to start using Microsoft Teams, the team owner can @ mention the person in conversations so that they receive notifications and are included in the collaboration efforts. Another great way team owners can support team members is by being available to answer questions. Team members are much more likely to use Microsoft Teams if they have someone to reach out to when they are confused or have questions. Good team owners can be excellent candidates to form a network of teamwork champions.

Teamwork Champions

A teamwork champion is someone from the business that cares about teamwork and is happy to help and share knowledge with colleagues on how to best use new tools and services, such as Teams. They can help the IT department drive user adoption from the business itself. Think of them as IT's eyes and ears out in the business, spreading the word and offering assistance to uncertain or willful colleagues and at the same time providing invaluable intel from the business back to the IT department and the rollout project.

When recruiting your teamwork champions to form a network of like-minded, it is a good strategy to start looking in the business pilot group. Look for people with different skills and background because diversity and inclusion are a real superpower that can truly increase the reach and impact teamwork champions have on user adoption. You probably already know of one or a few users that have showed ambassador skills, users that love to inspire others. Good, that's where you start. If you only look for the early adopters, you might be disappointed because they tend to be more focused on testing out new tools and technology rather than inspiring and helping others.

When you have formed the teamwork champions network, you need to treat them good; it is well-invested time and money that will pay off in the end.

To keep the engagement up, you need to have a plan. The main ingredients are not rocket science. Keep them updated through recurring meetings in Teams, both on what happens in the rollout project as well as new features and news about Microsoft Teams itself. The idea is also that champions should be super-user, and therefore, they need extra training and preferably some kind of support or mentoring from skilled people in the rollout project.

Then a little competition can sometimes be inspiring, like which department has the highest or fastest-growing Teams usage? Such things can drive the commitment and spur a champion to go the extra mile.

Teamwork champions are also a great group to distribute different models of Teams devices such as headsets and speakerphones, so users can check in and try different models and find their own favorite.

Keep a continuity in the activities, and make sure there is a mutual exchange, and you'll see that you get a crowd of raving Teams fans out in the organization who will help turn the rollout into a successful project.

Stop Duplication

A really big turn off for users is when they feel they have to perform a work function twice. This can happen when some users adopt Microsoft Teams but others haven't. An example is if a user uploads a document to a channel in Microsoft Teams and sends a message to a team member asking them to review it. The team member hasn't adopted Microsoft Teams and so never reads the message. The user then ends up having to email them the document and ask them again to review it. This is bound to happen during the early stages of a Microsoft Teams rollout, but it needs to be corrected, or there will be a lot of frustration. It may take leadership communicating that it is an expectation that everyone uses Microsoft Teams and reads their messages.

Check in with Users

It is a mistake to release Microsoft Teams to an organization and not frequently touch base with the users to receive feedback and answer any questions. This helps users feel supported and serves as a reminder to use it. Checking in with users is beneficial to increasing user adoption as long as actions are taken to improve user experiences based on feedback. All too often, users are experiencing issues and do not let anyone know because no one asks.

Let the Users Have Fun

The GIFs, stickers, and emojis in Microsoft Teams definitely offer a certain fun factor that most users enjoy. This can assist in fostering a positive culture where team members can express themselves. Unless there is a legitimate reason to disable or limit the GIFs and stickers, leave them be. If the GIFs and stickers are overused or become inappropriate, it may be only a few users that need guidance. If it is a widespread issue, then communicate guidance to all users and make adjustments to the settings if necessary. In Figure 5-2, you can see the authors having fun while writing this book.

Figure 5-2. *Having fun with Microsoft Teams*

Business Pilots

Microsoft Teams is a very flexible tool, which enables it to achieve many different business needs for chat, collaboration, and meetings. There are so many different ways that Microsoft Teams can be used, as well as settings and features that can be adjusted. Because of this, it is recommended to roll out Teams on a small scale first. Holding a Teams business pilot minimizes risk by providing a way to work out the specifics of your organizational culture, rather than impacting the entire organization.

The following are the benefits of doing a pilot:

- Determines the areas that users struggle with so that training can be the most beneficial

- Analyzes patterns in how the pilot group uses Microsoft Teams

- Receives the pilot group's feedback and turns it into actionable ways to improve the organization's experience with Microsoft Teams

- Excites a group of users who (hopefully) become champions and cheerleaders for Microsoft Teams

- Discovers any performance or security issues

- Resolves any technical issues, such as firewall configuration, application incompatibility, or authentication inconveniences that affect user experience

Choose one or a few projects, departments, or initiatives to use Microsoft Teams, and provide feedback before it goes to the masses so that you greatly increase the probability of successful user adoption. Elect the right group of people for a pilot is important. Generally, a good mix of skill levels and positive attitudes are the most important characteristics for a pilot group. Using the IT department for your pilot group may not represent how the rest of the organization will use the tool because IT professionals tend to be more knowledgeable about Microsoft Teams and are adept in implementing new software. You also don't want to choose a group that is too busy to provide feedback or use Microsoft Teams to its fullest potential.

The organization's size, culture, and technology skills determine the level of structure needed for the pilot. Providing some form of training to the pilot group before they start will give them the skills to make the most out of the pilot.

At a minimum, there should be a pilot kickoff meeting that outlines the pilot's

- Goals

- Expectations

- Schedule

- Success criteria

Training

Training is an essential part of user adoption. Microsoft Teams is very user-friendly, but even the most tech savvy of organizations should receive some training and guidance. Ideally, training would begin right before Microsoft Teams is rolled out in the organization. Users should also have access to training materials. There needs to be a clear path for users to get questions answered.

All users should have an understanding of the following concepts:

- How to access Microsoft Teams

- How to use teams and channels

- How to manage notifications

- How to chat and contribute to conversations

- How to share and access files

- How to schedule and attend meetings

- What tabs are and how to add them

Team owners have additional duties in Microsoft Teams that they need to be trained in. Ideally, team owners will also be available to answer questions from team members. It is important that team owners understand the differences in what a team owner can do in Microsoft Teams compared to someone in a team member role.

Team owners should have an understanding of these concepts:

- How to create, edit, and delete a team

- How to add team members and guests to a team

- How to manage team settings

Microsoft realized the importance of proper user training in how to use an application and is offering a very good collection of easy-to-use training videos within the Teams application itself. This is a great improvement over some past software that has been released.

To access the built-in Microsoft Teams training videos, select the Help icon found in the lower left-hand side corner in Microsoft Teams followed by Training, as is shown in Figure 5-3.

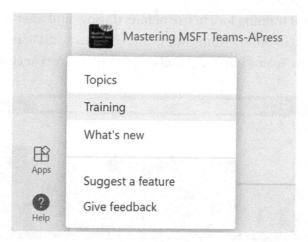

Figure 5-3. *Excellent built-in training videos available in Microsoft Teams*

Although these videos are very helpful, they may not cover all of the topics that the users need. In Chapter 6, you learn that creating a process for users to request a team might be a good idea. As a part of this process, you could add any custom training you feel is necessary for your users before they are allowed to use the team. Microsoft 365 learning pathways is such a tool where you can add custom training.

Microsoft 365 Learning Pathways

Microsoft 365 learning pathways is a free product training experience built on SharePoint Online, used by companies to drive adoption of Microsoft 365 applications including Microsoft Teams, SharePoint, and Office applications.

It is a SharePoint site that can be added into Teams as an app or tab within a channel, but also accessed as any other SharePoint site using a browser. Because it's built on SharePoint, it's customizable, and anyone who's ever edited a SharePoint page will recognize themselves instantly. There is a solid training content produced by Microsoft that is regularly updated automatically. In addition, it is possible to easily add your own training content and build your own so-called playlists with curated training material to suit the need for different categories of users and different workloads. An example of Microsoft 365 learning pathways when added as an app in Teams is shown in Figure 5-4.

Learning pathways is available in several languages and is also open for third-party educational partners to publish their own material to complement what already exists.

This is an excellent training tool to use before, during, and after a rollout project. If you want to get extra attention from your users, you can add Microsoft 365 learning pathways as an icon in Teams left tool panel and thus get direct access to the content.

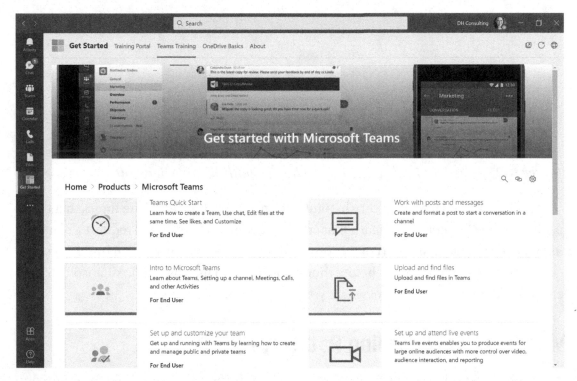

***Figure 5-4.** Sample Microsoft 365 learning pathways start page*

Note   Microsoft 365 learning pathways is not a learning management system as it does not keep track of who has undergone various training sessions and it does not generate such reports. If this is a requirement, have a look at Microsoft Viva Learning.

Microsoft 365 Adoption Resources

Microsoft understands that it's not just about building the best collaboration tools; organizations also need to be able to make the best use of the tools to get the most value out of the investments. That's why Microsoft has put together a portal with resources designed to help roll out Microsoft 365 services on a large scale. It's a collection of guides, tools, and best practices gathered from real-world implementations in collaboration with Microsoft partners and organizations that have gone through this already. The goal is to facilitate for other organizations by publishing best practices and tools from implementation projects, starting with the envision phase, via onboarding, to drive value over time.

Microsoft Teams is of course an important part of this, and there are plenty of great tools to facilitate the rollout of Microsoft Teams in organizations of different sizes and categories. But there are also guides and tools for other Microsoft 365 services such as SharePoint, Yammer, and Security & Compliance, which also play into the overall solution for a successful, productive, and secure organization.

The portal is well worth a visit or two, and the URL is `https://adoption.microsoft.com/`. Another great resource for Teams user adoption is Microsoft's "Tools for Driving Adoption" site that can be found here: `https://docs.microsoft.com/en-us/microsoftteams/adopt-tools-and-downloads`.

Swag

Take our word for it, there is nothing that drives user adoption of Microsoft Teams as well as Teams swag. It can be pretty much anything as long as it has a Microsoft Teams logo on it. If you should only bet on one thing, then go for stickers, works in all situations. The secret sauce is made of the Microsoft Teams logo together with a fun and important message about teamwork. It creates a must-have craving and provides a positive drive to the entire rollout. Try it, you will get amazed!

Ongoing Monitoring and Improvement

Adoption isn't always thought of as an ongoing process. Unfortunately, many organizations feel they do not have the resources or do not understand the impact of not implementing ongoing adoption. Like all software, the more it is used, the more you will find ways to improve how you interact with it. Over time, you may find that the software *stops* being used. There are almost always legitimate reasons why this occurs. It is important that someone is responsible for addressing the issue and resolving it to ensure long-term success with the application.

To help facilitate for ongoing monitoring as part of the overall adoption of Teams, Teams admin center holds usage reports for Teams usage. *To access these reports, you need to have your Office 365 administrator compile them for you or give you an admin role in the Office 365 admin center to allow you to create these reports yourself.*

There are several reports that can be processed for Microsoft Teams, including

- Microsoft Teams user activity

- Microsoft Teams device usage

- PSTN usage

The *user activity* report has detailed information on the number of channel messages, chat messages, calls, and meetings happening in the entire organization, as well as for individual users. From this data, you extract a number of different ideas on what might be happening in case long-term user adoption starts to fall off.

The good thing about these reports is that by listing the individual user's activity, you can quickly see which users might have been very active but suddenly their activity dropped. If a problem with long-term usage arises, you know which users to ask first about the problem. An example of this report is shown in Figure 5-5.

Figure 5-5. *Sample Teams user report for Microsoft Teams from the Teams admin center*

You (or your Office 365 administrator) have access to the Microsoft Teams Device Usage report. One benefit of this report is that it helps you realize the number of users accessing Microsoft Teams via different devices. Also, if a specific device's statistics suddenly trend downward, you can investigate the issue. An example of this report is shown in Figure 5-6.

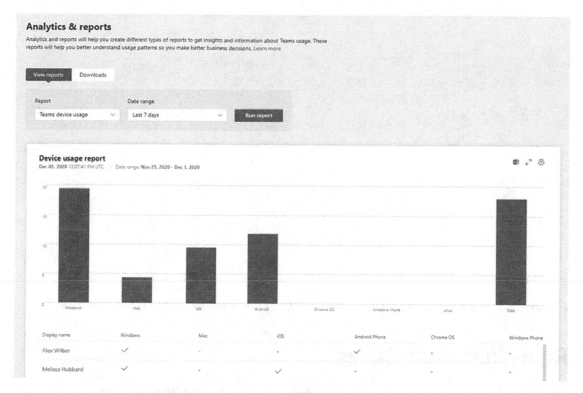

Figure 5-6. *Sample usage by device report for Teams from the Teams admin center*

Slightly simplified usage reports are also available in each team in Microsoft Teams, accessible to both team owners and members. These reports are great to track trends and general usage for the specific team. Select Manage team, and click the Analytics tab to view the report. An example of this report is shown in Figure 5-7.

Figure 5-7. Sample usage report available in each team in Microsoft Teams

Real-World Use Cases

The following are some examples of how Microsoft Teams can be used to maximize the benefits the app has to offer. It is important to remember that every organization is different, and Microsoft Teams may fit into the information technology strategy in various ways.

Note   Schools have access to additional team templates and features that are not covered here.

Use Case 1: Coordinating a New Initiative

A nonprofit organization is starting a new initiative to educate children about healthy eating in impoverished schools. It creates a private team and adds everyone that is working on the initiative as team members. A channel is added for each of the four schools the initiative is targeting. Within those channels, the team members discuss their lesson plans, creation of materials, scheduling, and other topics related to the particular school. They use the documents tab in these channels to store the customized learning materials and forms that they created for each school. The team members that are assigned to each school favorite the channel for that particular school to make sure that they stay up to date on channel activities. The General channel is used to discuss topics that apply to the overall initiative, such as funding and team assignments. A tab is set up showing a Power BI chart displaying metrics on the number of students that have participated in the initiative from each school. A OneNote notebook is added as a Tab and outlines the protocols that should be followed when team members arrive at a school. Team members often use channel conversations to quickly and transparently reach a consensus about planning decisions. A sample of the channel structure is seen in Figure 5-8.

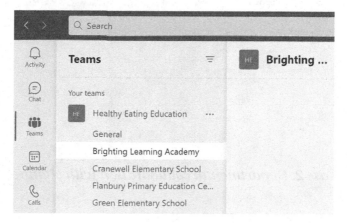

Figure 5-8. *Use Case 1: Coordinating a project with channels*

Use Case 2: Departmental Collaboration

The Human Resources department of a large enterprise has a private team created for them by the IT department. Channels are set up for the different functions and activities of the department, such as recruitment, benefits, payroll, and training.

The General channel contains a tab for the benefits service that the whole team uses regularly in their workday. The recruitment channel has tabs for Microsoft Lists where recruitment possibilities are stored, as well as a tab containing a Microsoft Word document that is regularly referred to for guidance when cold-calling recruits. The training channel is primarily used to discuss the training materials being developed.

Team members use a tab containing a Microsoft Excel document that the organization uses to track employees' mandatory training requirements. The benefits channel stores many documents from benefits vendors that are distributed to staff. The team holds weekly meetings in the benefits channel to discuss any new updates and issues. The payroll channel is a private channel that only a subset of the team members have been given access to, because of the sensitive information being shared within that channel. A private channel is marked with a lock symbol indicating that this is a private channel. Team members that are not part of the channel Payroll won't see the channel.

They use Yammer to connect people and information across the organization. You can see the channel structure of this use case in Figure 5-9.

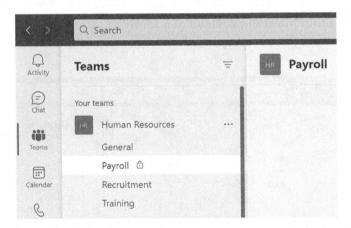

Figure 5-9. *Use Case 2: Departmental collaboration with channels*

Use Case 3: Managing IT Projects

A small IT consulting company has 40 staff members spread out in several different countries and who all work from home. They have five large long-term clients for which they provide IT solutions and support. In Microsoft Teams, they have a separate team for each client because they do not want staff members viewing the content of a client they are not working with.

Each team has one or more external contacts added as guests; it can be subcontractors or vendors collaborating on the specific client. Project managers use a tab in the project management channel to display the Planner app in Office 365, where they assign and track tasks. They also schedule daily stand-up meetings in Microsoft Teams, track attendance, and ask for updates in respective channel.

The testing channels are used by the quality assurance team members. They discuss testing activities and schedules. Also, they contain a tab to a quality log that is in Microsoft Lists. The development channels have tabs displaying Visual Studio Team Services, which is a tool the developers use as a code repository and to track bugs. They often hold meetings where they share their screens and do code reviews.

Summary

Hopefully, the biggest takeaway from this chapter is that adoption and long-term success with Microsoft Teams in your organization is not something you should expect happened by itself or think it will take just a small amount of time and effort. It may not be easy to implement all of these strategies and ideas or find stakeholders to take on the responsibility to own them, but at least you will know that if you do not perform the tasks at hand, your odds of success will be a lot less than those who have. In the next chapter, we discuss how to govern Microsoft Teams within your organization. User adoption and governance go hand in hand, because if your deployment of Microsoft Teams lacks governance, then performance and functionality suffer, which ultimately turns off your users.

CHAPTER 6

Governance

Governance goes hand in hand with user adoption. Having a well-thought-out governance plan ensures that Microsoft Teams is managed and used in the way it was intended. Users will adopt Microsoft Teams if it is well governed and useful to them. A solid governance plan ensures that the user experience remains positive and that organization assets are stored and used properly. The biggest selling point of Microsoft Teams is that it improves the speed and ease of collaboration by providing one location where teammates can interact, share content, and conduct meetings. However, the benefits will only be realized if time is spent planning the administration and management of the service prior to making it available to your users. Without a governance plan, there are pitfalls that will negate these benefits.

This chapter discusses the essential areas of governance for Microsoft Teams to consider and offer practical advice. Real-world examples and explanations help you build a governance plan that ensures that content is secure and that Microsoft Teams is convenient and easy to use, thus driving user adoption.

Creating Your Own Plan

Creating your own governance plan for Microsoft Teams should, at the very least, include the following items:

- How to organize the structure of your team (this could be different for each team you create)

- How to allow people to request or create a new team (a process for creating Teams)

- How to determine if there should be a new team created

© Melissa Hubbard, Matthew J. Bailey, D'arce Hess, Mårten Hellebro 2021
M. Hubbard et al., *Mastering Microsoft Teams*, https://doi.org/10.1007/978-1-4842-6898-8_6

- Understanding options to archive old or unused teams

- When a Team should be deleted

- Features and organizational settings

Now let's go into more detail for each bullet point so that you can create your own governance plan.

Organizational Structure for Teams and Channels

Microsoft Teams can easily become unmanageable if it is rolled out with the default settings, and users have no guidance. By default, all users can create new teams and channels. One parallel that many IT professionals can draw upon is the structure of SharePoint. Before the importance of governance was realized, many users were given access to create new sites at their discretion. Without proper training, planning, and strategizing about when to create new sites, there quickly became an uncontrollable environment. The lack of governance harmed user adoption of SharePoint; let's use the lessons learned to avoid this happening with Microsoft Teams.

It is very important to analyze your organization's work functions, departments, products, initiatives, and/or projects to strategize how to lay out teams and channels. A key point to remember is that permissions can only be set at the team level. Until Microsoft releases secure channels, all content in channels is open and available to all members of the team that the channel is part of.

Tip   When strategizing the organizational structure of teams and channels, it is very important to consider who should have access to what content.

Figure 6-1 shows an example of an organizational structure where a team is created for each major department, including each office that falls under the department with a channel.

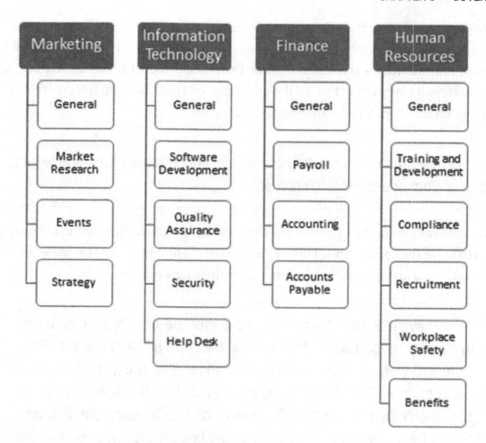

Figure 6-1. *Teams organization by department*

As you can see, the Information Technology department has a team with channels for the Help Desk, Software Development, Quality Assurance, and Security offices. The General channel is used for department-wide communication and file sharing. Each office uses their channel for communication and collaboration. This organizational structure makes sense in theory, but if the Security office is communicating about confidential topics in their conversations tab, all the other offices will be able to read it. In a situation like this, each office needs its own team.

Note   If needed, private channels could be used if only a smaller subset of users should have access.

Now imagine if all of the offices were already heavily using their channel in the Information Technology team by having conversations, holding meetings, and uploading files. After four months, it is realized that the team needs to be broken up so that each office can have its own team. But, all the conversations and meeting information from the offices' channels cannot be moved to their teams.

Note   Conversations and meeting content cannot be moved from one team to another or from one channel to another.

The only option for the offices to see their content in the Information Technology team is to leave the team active. This can lead to confusion and error because the offices may accidently use their old channel instead of their new team.

Tip   If you have to leave a team that is no longer used, but team members still need to access the existing content, rename the team and add a description to indicate that there should be nothing new added. For example, "Information Technology team—READ ONLY." In the description, let users know which team they should be using instead. You can also consider using the archiving functionality found under the "gear" icon in the bottom left corner of your Teams interface, and then select the team you would like to archive.

Figure 6-2 shows an organization that has organized teams by project. It is common for organizations to create a team for every project, client, or case that they work on. This is different than organizing by department because there is usually a definitive start and end in these scenarios. Having this structure makes sense for when there are different people working on every project, client, or case, especially if they need to invite external guest users to collaborate with. If a law firm is using Microsoft Teams to collaborate on files and hold conversations about a case, they may want to invite the client to view files in Teams and discuss the case. It is important that they only have access to their own case, not that of others. A separate team per case is the only way to achieve this.

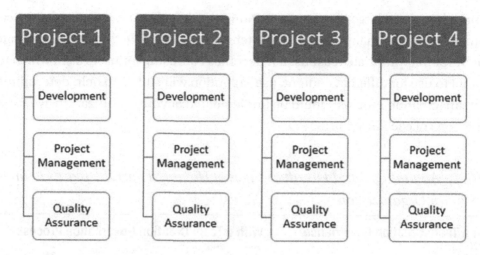

Figure 6-2. *Teams organization by project*

There is no one blueprint for the Microsoft Teams organizational structure that can be used for all organizations. Not properly planning how teams and channels will be organized can severely damage user adoption. It can also put an organization at risk of having sensitive or private content accessed by the wrong people. An analysis of the different work functions of an organization and gaining insight into who is sharing and collaborating on different types of content will help you plan for success. As discussed in Chapter 5, holding a pilot prior to the rollout to the entire organization empowers you in this analysis.

Process for Creating and Managing Teams

Planning the team's organizational structure is the first step. No matter how well you plan, governing the team's organizational structure is an ongoing duty. The next step is to decide how new teams are created and the process to manage it.

Restricting Who Can Create Teams

By default, everyone can create a team. This has both pros and cons. Allowing everyone to be able to create a team allows for fluidity of work and an agile approach for organizations. Small organizations that are technologically savvy may be able to get away with leaving the default team creation setting by providing guidance on when it is appropriate to create a new team.

For medium- and large-sized organizations, the default team creation setting can be problematic. With too many cooks in the kitchen, it is inevitable that a team is created in error or for inappropriate reasons. If it becomes confusing for users as to which team or channel to use for different content, user adoption will suffer. To help determine if a formal team creation process should be implemented at your organization, we list the pros and cons of each in Table 6-1.

Table 6-1. *Advantages and Disadvantages of Having a Formal Teams Request Process in an Organization*

Without a Team Creation Governance Process	With a Team Creation Governance Process
Promotes adoption and usage	Could limit user adoption
Allows users to make a team what they want it to be	Might restrict the ways users can interact and utilize teams
Creates massive sprawl with difficulties managing and taking up storage space	Prevents "teams sprawl," which saves SharePoint and other services storage space
Doesn't follow naming conventions	Allows for understandable naming conventions
Possible issues with classification and the types of data being stored in the team	Allows for classification and tracking information about the team
Prevents users from agreeing to a term of service or required training	Can affect other Office 365 applications that rely on groups (planner)
Hard to determine what teams you have in your environment (may change)	Allows IT administrators to manage and monitor teams in the organization
Doesn't guarantee an administrator is an owner of a team	Allows you to place an administration group as a team owner
Allows for duplicate team names, which can create confusion for everyone	Prevents duplicate naming
Consistent URLs could be taken and content would be inconsistent with overarching strategy	Allows for department or function names to align with the business and URLs to be provisioned appropriately

---

Note   Team members can only be restricted to create channels at the team level. There is no setting in the Office 365 admin center to restrict channel permissions.

As you can see in Table 6-1, most reasoning leans toward implementing a team creation and governance process at an organization. To restrict team creation, an Office 365 administrator needs to run PowerShell commands. One issue with this is that to restrict someone from creating a new team, you have to restrict them from creating a new group in Office 365. This is because when you create a new team, it creates a group. Restricting someone from creating a group also prevents them from creating a team. Obviously, if there is a strong business need for everyone to be able to create groups or Planners in Office 365, you will not be able to restrict them from creating teams.

Note   In order to restrict someone from creating teams, you need to restrict them from creating groups in Office 365.

Process for Creating Teams

If the decision is made to restrict who can create a team, you need to determine a process for how teams are created. There are several options for how this can be handled. What is best can be vastly different from one organization to another.

If the creation of new teams is restricted to a small group of collaboration specialists or IT professionals, users will need a quick and easy process to request new teams. If the process is not clear, or is cumbersome or takes too long, users will find work-arounds to get their jobs done. They could begin using an existing team inappropriately to collaborate on content unrelated to the rest of the Teams' content, or they could begin collaborating in a different tool outside of Teams. Once a group of people gets in a work rhythm, it is difficult to change their habits and bring them back to using Teams.

If an organization already has a well-established ticketing system, this may be the best option. It is imperative that end users clearly know how to specifically request a new team. Teams-related requests and questions need to be quickly routed to the collaboration specialists or IT professionals that specialize in Teams. Open lines of communication between those that create the teams and the end users requesting them are necessary.

If an organization does not have an existing ticketing or help desk system, some mechanism for users to request a team needs to be developed. One suggestion is to use a SharePoint list that everyone in the organization has access to. Figure 6-3 shows an example of a SharePoint list form to request a new team. There should be fields for users to enter the name of the team that they are requesting. It is also important that they provide a reason for needing the team. This helps determine if the team is actually necessary. Team owners of the new team should be included in the request. Also, it is important to find out if external guest users will be part of the proposed team.

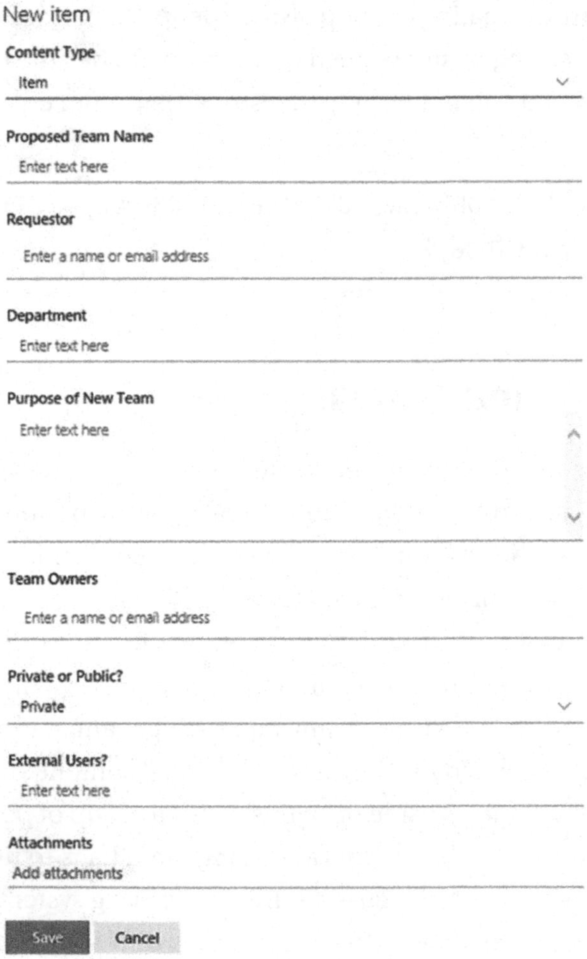

New item

Content Type
> Item   ⌄

Proposed Team Name
> Enter text here

Requestor
> Enter a name or email address

Department
> Enter text here

Purpose of New Team
> Enter text here   ⌃
>
>   ⌄

Team Owners
> Enter a name or email address

Private or Public?
> Private   ⌄

External Users?
> Enter text here

Attachments
> Add attachments

[Save]   [Cancel]

Figure 6-3. *Example SharePoint form allowing users to request a new team*

Because there are so many different ways that an organization could implement a Teams creation process, in the next section, we explain many of the concepts you could use as a process. There is no magic answer on which process to select. Evaluating the pros and cons of each and matching them to your organization's needs will help you decide which option to pursue.

Teams Creation Options

In this section, we present the options and their pros and cons.

No Team Creation Process

Just "flipping the switch" to turn on Microsoft Teams without any planning or consideration is not an option for most organizations. Unless you have no concerns about the data, we do not advise taking this approach. Noting this, the following states the pros and cons.

Pros

This approach promotes the greatest short-term adoption possibilities, requires little planning or training, and is the fastest to implement.

Cons

The negative consequences of this process are great if you have any need to retain, organize, sort, manage, or reuse your data over a period of time. Later in this chapter, we explain many of the negative effects the process could have.

Team Request Reviewed by Admin or Help Desk

One scenario of a team creation process is implementing a team request process by using a new form or list within an existing team to request a team from within the Teams client. An admin, help desk, or IT teams specialist reviews the requests and then creates the team if it is approved.

Pros

The pros of this solution are that it is quick to implement, and there is no additional cost for the organization. Configuration of the SharePoint list could prevent users from submitting a duplicate team name.

Cons

This process requires a human to process each request, which takes time and resources. It also requires you to turn off the ability to create groups for your users and only allow certain persons to create new groups and teams.

Placing Teams Requestors in a Security Group

This approach is another recommendation by Microsoft. It could be considered a "meet us in the middle" idea. To implement it, you need your Office 365 administrator to create a security group and only place persons you trust in this group. You could ensure that the users have completed training before placing them in this group.

Pros

The pros of this approach are that it frees up time for your IT administrators or help desk by letting trusted users create teams themselves. It also allows those persons to create other related Office 365 applications such as Planners, Yammer groups, and Office 365 groups without further interaction from others.

Cons

This process doesn't guarantee that the people you place in the security group will follow all of your rules. If you have naming conventions, or you want to prevent duplicate names, or you want to restrict the number of teams created due to space and organizational requirements, the users may not abide by the rules.

SharePoint Request List That Triggers a Flow

If you are looking for an idea that completely restricts users from creating teams (and any other groups-related applications), this concept is the least programmatic way to accomplish the task. It requires setting up a SharePoint list, which you program to perform any checks that you need before the user submits the list item. Upon the list item being submitted, you trigger a flow that will work to provision the associated Team.

Pros

The advantages of this approach are controlling the number, naming, and frequency of new teams. It also requires a bit less programming than the upcoming final suggestion. It is almost immediate and doesn't require your users to wait for the new team to be created.

Cons

The disadvantages of this approach are that it takes time to create and requires someone who has some technical knowledge. It also requires that your organization has approved the flow to use, and it could end up with additional costs if you have run a very large number of requests. Finally, if you have any needs to customize the components that create a team (i.e., making alterations to the SharePoint site collection to disable external sharing), you will not be able to do so. The restriction that users have to request any application that is group-based also applies.

SharePoint Request List with PowerShell or Code

This idea is the most intricate of any we have discussed. However, if you are in a very rigid organization that demands structure, governance, and control, this approach will suit you the best. The idea starts with a user requesting a team from a SharePoint list, and then either a scheduled task on a Windows server or Azure Functions processes the list items, creates the team, and notifies the requestor.

Pros

The advantage of this method is that it controls your team down to the greatest detail. You could customize your team (within the parameters that Microsoft allows) to appear in a certain way, or to have certain users in it. You could also alter attached components, such as SharePoint site collection sharing settings. If you need to track other information about the team, or to create an annual review process, it can also be done.

Cons

The downside of this approach is that it requires a skilled programmer to create. You also need either an Azure account or a Windows server to run the code on. If you choose to set the code on a schedule, your users will experience a delay before they can use the team. The restriction that users must request any application that is group based also applies.

If all of these ideas seem too time-consuming and difficult, you can search the Internet for a third-party application that automates it. These products usually cost a great deal and need to be thoroughly investigated before purchasing.

Determining If a New Team Should Be Created

When reviewing a request for a new team, there are a few factors that you should consider in determining whether the team should be created. Primarily, you want to make sure that you avoid duplication by creating a team that already exists. You also want to avoid creating too many teams. Duplication makes it confusing and frustrating for end users. Having a large number of teams creates a hassle for users that are receiving too many notifications and having to switch between teams all day to get work done. If external guest users need to be included on a team, a new team will be needed. The reason is that, typically, external guests are not able to access any team content outside of the work they are performing. Even if the proposed new team could be a channel under an existing team, if external guests shouldn't be able to access the rest of the team channels, a new team has to be created.

When deciding if a new Team should be created, ask yourself the following questions:

- Does a team or channel already exist for the same department, initiative, project, case, or account?

- Does a team already exist that has the same members as the proposed team?

- Are external guest team members going to be included?

Process for Creating and Managing Channels

Teams provides the unique ability to have a nested structure that provides the parent Team as well as Channels that can be created within the Team. Channels are the focus of where work is done within the Team.

Types of Channels

There are two types of channels within Teams. The first is a public channel. This type of channel is open to anyone who has been added as a member of the general Team. By default, all members of the Team have the ability to create new channels within the Team.

Public Channels

Public channels such as the General channel are available to all members of the Team. These types of channels can be created by any member of the team as long as the team owner has allowed this in the team settings. These channels will show under the General channel which is the default channel for each team created.

How Public Channels Can Be Used

Public channels can be used to break up a workstream within a project or a team. An example may be a project team that will have multiple workstreams such as having a team of analysts, a team of developers, and a team of leads or managers. One example that may be used is to create a channel for each of the roles on the team, so that the members of those channels can focus on the work that is directed toward them without needing to sort through a larger set of messages and content from all of the workstreams.

Another example can be breaking up a project to a specific set of phases such as Discovery, Design, Implementation, Quality Assurance, and Deployment. Each of these workstreams may have specific documents related to it, different conversations, and, in some cases, may have different members that will join or leave the project.

Private Channels

Private channels offer the opportunity for a limited subset of users within a Team to have a private area to collaborate or share sensitive information such as budgets or strategic plans. Private channels should be used sparingly as each Team is limited in the number of private channels. When a private channel is created, it will also provision a separate site collection where documents are stored. Anyone may access the information stored within a private channel as long as that person or guest is a member of the Team and has been invited into the private channel. Any Team owner or member can create a private channel. Guest user does not have the ability to create private channels, but may be invited to join a private channel.

Who Should Be Able to Create Private Channels?

The ability to create private channels can be managed from an organizational level as well as a team level. In order to control the ability to create private channels from the organizational level, the Team's Administrator can set up a policy in the Teams Admin Center. Custom policies may take a couple of hours to take effect.

From a Team perspective, the member of the Team that creates the private channel becomes the owner of the private channel. The private channel owner is the only person who can invite others to the private channel, including guests.

Roles and Responsibilities

As with any process or system, assigning roles and responsibilities is essential. With Teams, there are primary roles that need to be assigned and communicated to make sure that there is accountability. These roles are decision maker, Office 365 administrator, team owner, and team member.

Decision Maker

There are decisions regarding Teams that need to be made on an ongoing basis. This includes decisions about implementation, configuration, integration with other applications, and processes for creating teams and channels. If an organization decides to limit who can create teams, the decision maker may be in charge of determining whether a team should be created or not. Many large organizations have created governance boards to provide technical leadership and make decisions regarding the use of collaboration tools and their maintenance. We have witnessed SharePoint governance boards kill collaboration and user adoption due to taking too long to make decisions and for micromanaging SharePoint to the point that it was unusable.

When leadership and IT staff, who are usually part of these boards, are too busy or are uninterested in being involved, it slows down collaboration and thus hurts user adoption. In some cases, an official governance board is necessary due to an organizational policy, or the governance board model is successful for decision making on other collaboration tools.

Another option for decision making is to designate specialists to facilitate and expedite collaboration and serve as the liaison between end users, team owners, and Office 365 administrators. These collaboration specialists should have thorough knowledge of Teams, as well as any other collaboration tools that the organization uses. A collaboration specialist ensures that questions and requests are handled promptly.

Office 365 Administrator

Office 365 administrators have access to the Microsoft Teams tenant-wide settings. It is their job to provide technical administration guidance and support. They are also responsible for any performance-related issues experienced when using Microsoft Teams. The administrator will have the role to implement governance policies and security features to protect the organization and the users. The administrator will also control which apps will be allowed for integration with Teams.

Team Owner

Team owners have the important responsibility of leading a team. Team owners monitor the content and make sure that it is appropriate and productive. Team owners also have several settings that they can change for the team and directly impact the experience team members have when working in the team. Teams allows for up to one hundred team owners per team. In most cases, we recommend having at least two team owners, but not more than four. Having any more than this will most likely lead to confusion and aggravation. Team owners should always stay in close communication with one another so that everyone is on the same page, especially when changing settings, which are discussed later in this chapter. Team members always need to know who the team owners are so that they know where to go for a first line of support and questions. Team owners hold the responsibility of inviting new members to a team and also remove members.

Team Member

Team members can be part of one or many teams. Anyone in an organization assigned a Teams license can be a team member. Team members are responsible for staying current on their work. They have the responsibility to discuss and work on the appropriate content for the team and channel. They also need to understand how to follow and favorite teams and channels so that their notifications are effective. A team member may have the opportunity to create a private channel within a team and should have an understanding of which type of channel and the correct audience before proceeding.

Feature Review

Remarkably, much of the functionality in Microsoft Teams can be changed and customized. Some of the feature customization is done at the team level and some at the organizational level. Team owners have the ability to customize their team's features and member permissions in the team settings. The vast power team owners have to shape the user experience is just one more reason that it is critical to choose the right team owners and train them.

Office 365 administrators can use tenant-wide settings to change and customize the features for all teams. Some settings can be set at both the team level and the organizational level. It is important to know that the tenant-wide settings always take priority over the team settings.

Note   You can customize Teams features at both the organizational level and the team level, but the organizational settings always take precedence.

Organizational Settings

An organization's Teams experience and features can be customized using the Office 365 admin center tenant-wide settings. Every organization has unique business needs and scenarios. Teams is built in a way that much of the functionality can be enabled or disabled in an a la carte fashion. Holding a pilot helps establish which features should be enabled or disabled in an organization. Once Teams is rolled out to everyone in the organization, everyone becomes accustomed to the functionalities. End users will be unhappy if features get removed after they have already started using them. For this reason, it is important for Teams administrators to perform a review of the feature settings in the Office 365 admin center. It is important that the Teams administrator with a member on the business side help communicate upcoming changes and help with the change management process to prepare users for new functionality that may be coming as well as retiring functionality.

To review Teams tenant-wide settings in the Microsoft Teams admin center

1. Select the Teams admin center from the Admin centers list, as shown in Figure 6-4.

2. Select **Microsoft Teams** from the list.

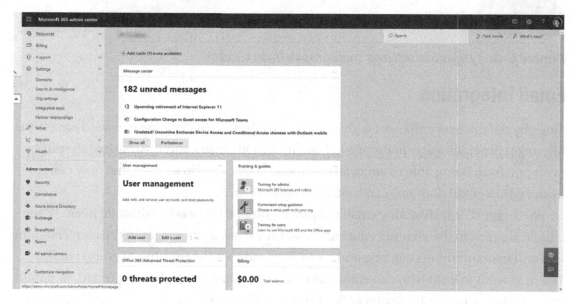

Figure 6-4. *Admin Center selection with Microsoft Teams Admin Center*

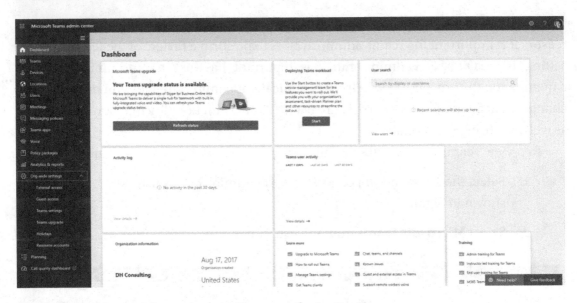

Figure 6-5. *Org-wide settings in Teams Admin Center*

Email Integration

Since by default every channel is given an email address that anyone can send emails to, Microsoft provides a way to disable or limit them. Office 365 administrators can restrict everyone from being able to email all channels. They can also set it so that only people from certain email domains can send channel emails.

We suggest only disabling email to every channel if there is a legitimate need. When emails are sent to the channel email address, they show as messages in the conversations tab, and team members can respond there. This reduces the number of group emails. You may want to limit who can email the channel if you start getting spammed, or emails become distracting or irrelevant to the work (see Figure 6-6).

Email integration

Email integration lets people send an email to a Teams channel, and have the contents of the email displayed in the conversations for all team members to view.

Allow users to send emails to a channel email address	🔵 On
Accept channel email from these SMTP domains	Press the space bar after you enter a domain.

Figure 6-6. *Email integration settings in the Office 365 admin center*

External Apps and Cloud Storage

Microsoft Teams has the capability to connect with other apps. When creating tabs in channels, these apps can be selected so that users can work with them without having to leave the Microsoft Teams app. Office 365 admins can disable the use of any external apps, as seen in Figure 6-7. They can also pick and choose which apps should be allowed.

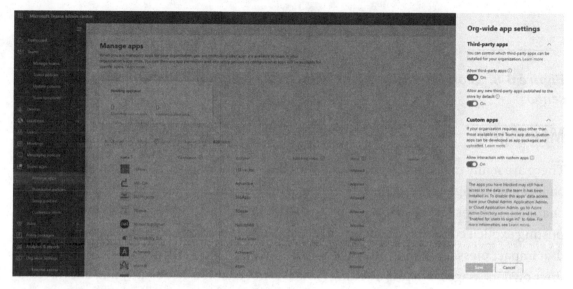

Figure 6-7. *Apps settings in the Office 365 admin center*

Cloud Storage

Cloud storage options outside of Office 365, such as Google Drive or Dropbox, can be configured to allow uploading and sharing files. Office 365 administrators can choose to disable all cloud storage options or to only keep some enabled. We see an example of these settings in Figure 6-8.

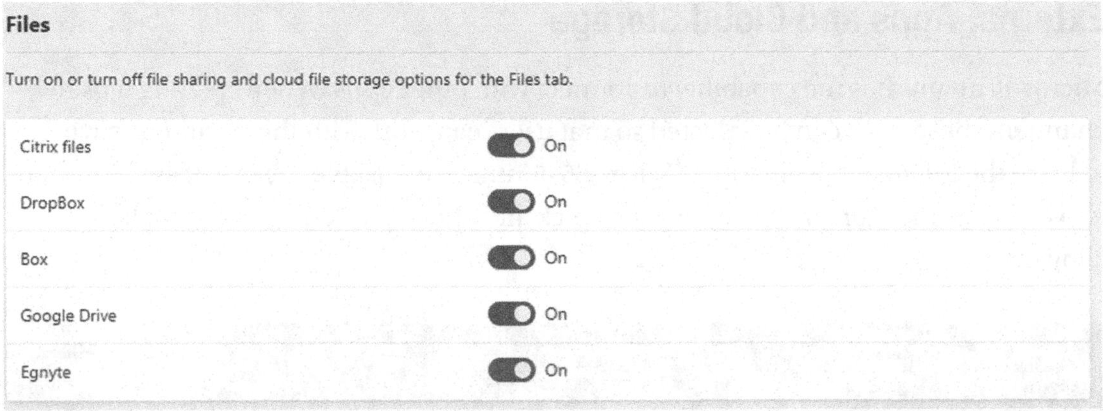

Files

Turn on or turn off file sharing and cloud file storage options for the Files tab.

Citrix files	⬤◯	On
DropBox	⬤◯	On
Box	⬤◯	On
Google Drive	⬤◯	On
Egnyte	⬤◯	On

Figure 6-8. *Cloud storage options in the Teams settings in the Office 365 admin center*

Messaging

There are many messaging options that the Office 365 administrator can change. Private chat can be completely disabled. The messaging experience can be customized by changing options for memes, stickers, and GIFs. The content rating can be changed if posting explicit content is a concern. The important messaging settings are the ones that impact message editing and deletion. By default, users can edit and delete all of their own messages. There is a setting (which is not enabled by default) that allows team owners to delete all messages, as seen in Figure 6-9. There may be a need to turn this on if there are a lot of "fluff" messages in a team. This setting should be enabled with caution, and team owners should receive training and guidance on this.

Owners can delete sent messages	⬤ Off
Delete sent messages	⬤ On
Edit sent messages	⬤ On
Read receipts	User controlled ⌄
Chat ⓘ	⬤ On
Use Giphys in conversations	⬤ On
Giphy content rating	Moderate ⌄
Use Memes in conversations	⬤ On
Use Stickers in conversations	⬤ On
Allow URL previews	⬤ On
Translate messages	⬤ On
Allow immersive reader for viewing messages	⬤ On
Send urgent messages using priority notifications ⓘ	⬤ On
Create voice messages	Allowed in chats and channels ⌄
On mobile devices, display favorite channels above recent chats	Disabled ⌄
Remove users from group chats	⬤ On
Suggested replies ⓘ	⬤ On

Figure 6-9. *Messaging settings in the Teams in the Teams admin center*

Calls and Meetings

Private, channel, and ad hoc meetings can all be disabled. If an organization already has a method for holding virtual meetings that users have adopted, and it is working well, it may be a good idea to disable meetings in Teams in order to avoid confusion. An organization may have issues with allowing video and screen sharing in meetings if there are any bandwidth or security policies prohibiting it. These options can be disabled, as seen in Figure 6-10. Private calling is another option that can be disabled if necessary.

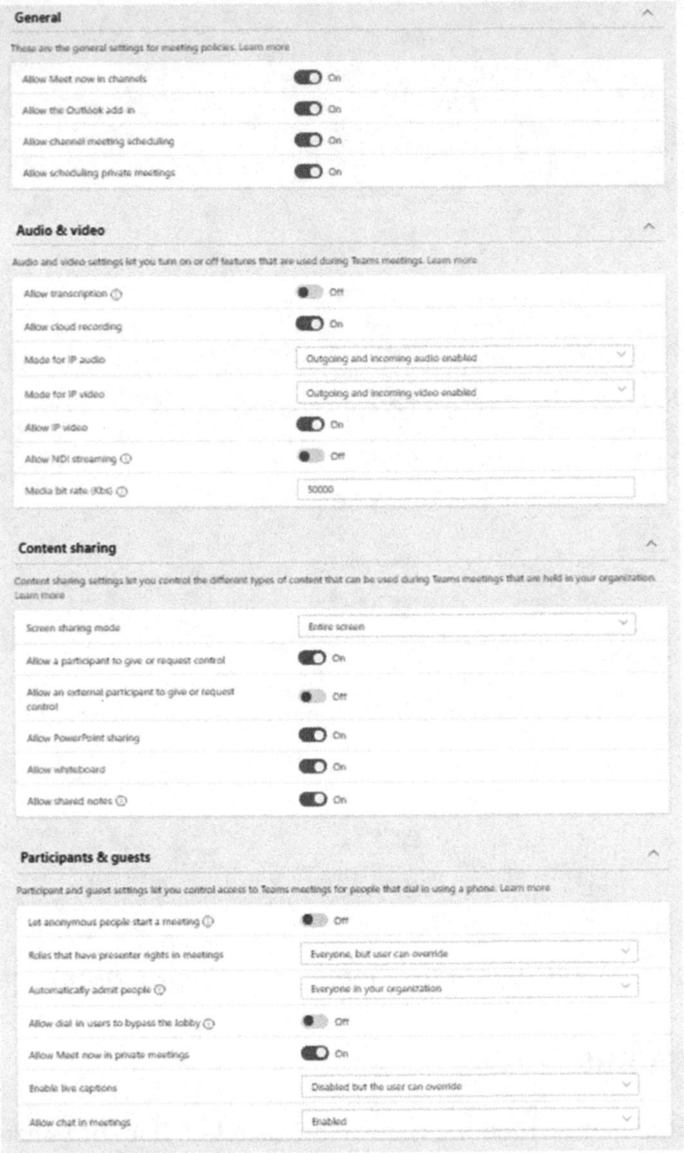

Figure 6-10. *Calls and meeting settings in the Office 365 admin center*

External Users

Teams allows external users to collaborate with team members. There is a common business need to invite clients, subcontractors, vendors, and consultants to view team files and hold conversations within Teams. Many agencies have privacy concerns about allowing external users within Teams. To keep external users out of Teams, Office 365 administrators can select Guest as the license type, and then turn off Teams as the users of that type (see Figure 6-11).

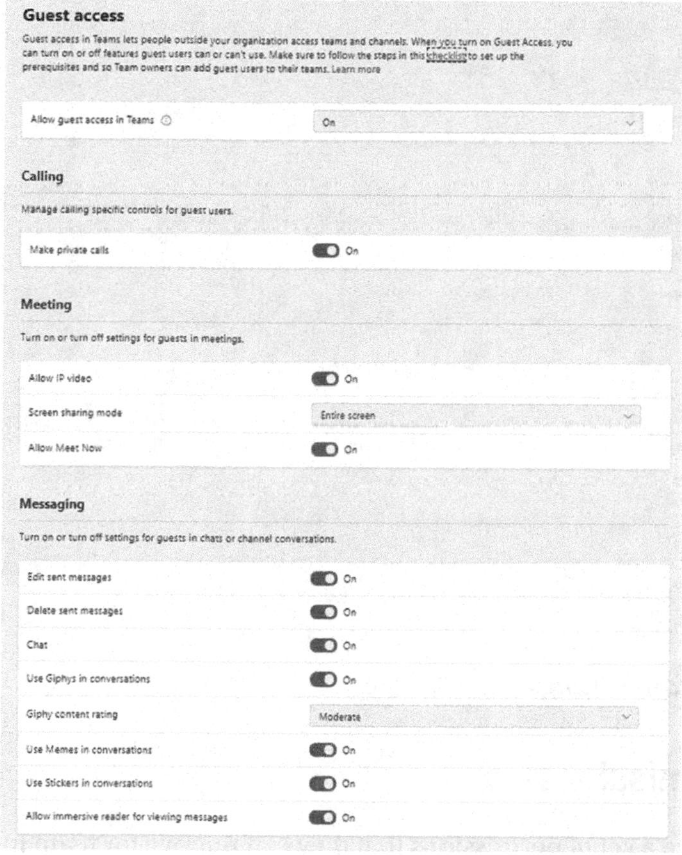

Figure 6-11. *Preventing external users from accessing a team in the Office 365 admin center*

Team-Level Settings

Team owners can customize how their team is used by changing the team settings. Team member and guest permissions can be changed, as well as the ability to mention teams and channels, and the "fun" settings, which include emojis, memes, and GIFs. These settings do not impact any other teams.

It is important that team members know to only change these settings if there is a need. Team owners should communicate any setting changes to end users so that they are not surprised when they are unable to do something.

Members Channels Settings Analytics Apps	
▸ **Team picture**	Add a team picture
▸ **Member permissions**	Enable channel creation, adding apps, and more
▸ **Guest permissions**	Enable channel creation
▸ **@mentions**	Choose who can use @team and @channel mentions
▸ **Team code**	Share this code so people can join the team directly - you won't get join requests
▸ **Fun stuff**	Allow emoji, memes, GIFs, or stickers
▸ **Tags**	Choose who can manage tags

Figure 6-12. *Team settings*

Member Permissions

Team owners have a set of permissions that they can remove for team members. Permissions are set for all team members. There is no way to grant some team members different permissions than other team members, except for guest members. For large or not technologically savvy teams, we recommend removing the ability to create, update, delete, and restore channels, apps, tabs, and connectors. These actions should be performed at the team owner's discretion. Some organizations may wish to remove the permissions of team members to delete and/or edit their messages. Be very cautious about changing these settings because team members will be much less likely to use the conversation functionality in Teams if the know they can't edit typos or delete messages written in error or that they change their mind about. Figure 6-13 illustrates these settings.

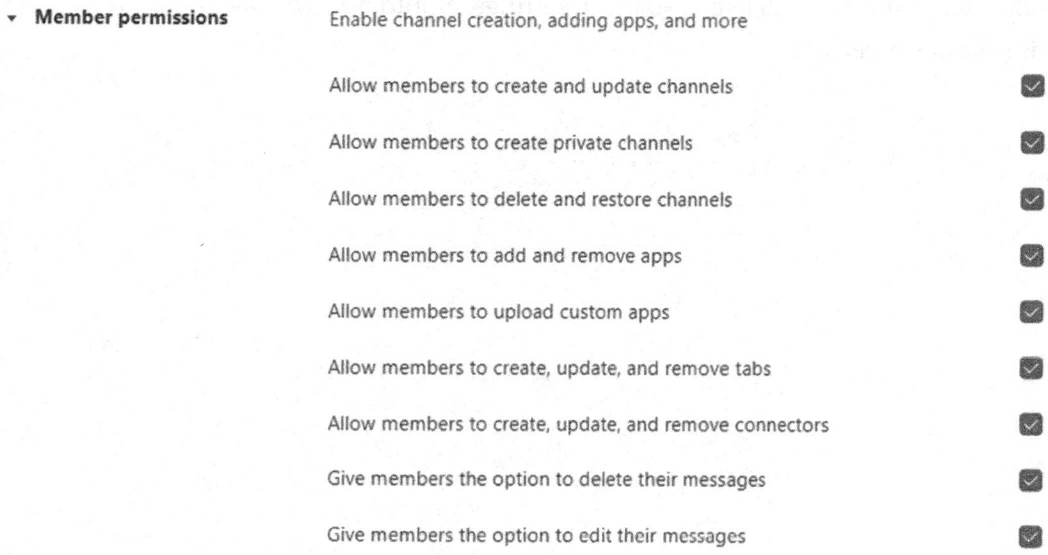

▼ **Member permissions**   Enable channel creation, adding apps, and more

     Allow members to create and update channels   ☑

     Allow members to create private channels   ☑

     Allow members to delete and restore channels   ☑

     Allow members to add and remove apps   ☑

     Allow members to upload custom apps   ☑

     Allow members to create, update, and remove tabs   ☑

     Allow members to create, update, and remove connectors   ☑

     Give members the option to delete their messages   ☑

     Give members the option to edit their messages   ☑

Figure 6-13. *Member permissions settings*

Guest Permissions

There is the ability to grant guest team members permissions for creating, updating, and deleting channels. By default, this is disabled, because there are few situations where guests need or should have this control.

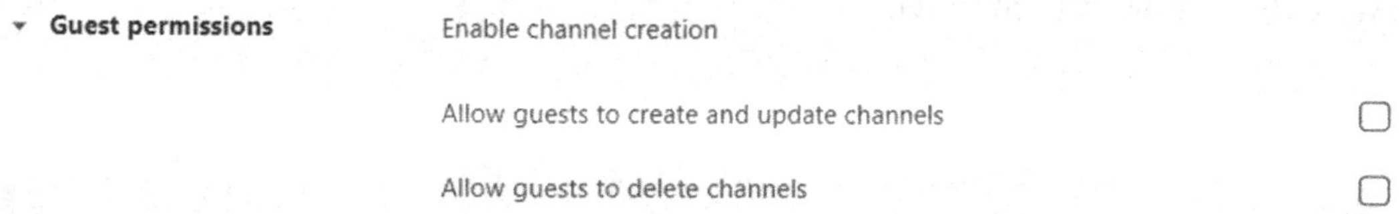

▼ **Guest permissions**   Enable channel creation

     Allow guests to create and update channels   ☐

     Allow guests to delete channels   ☐

Figure 6-14. *Guest permission settings*

Email Integration

Email settings are configurable on a per channel basis, as seen in Figure 6-15. It is possible to restrict only team members or email addresses from within certain domains so as to be able to email the channel address. Changing the email settings for only a few channels confuses end users, so these settings should only be touched if there is a specific business reason.

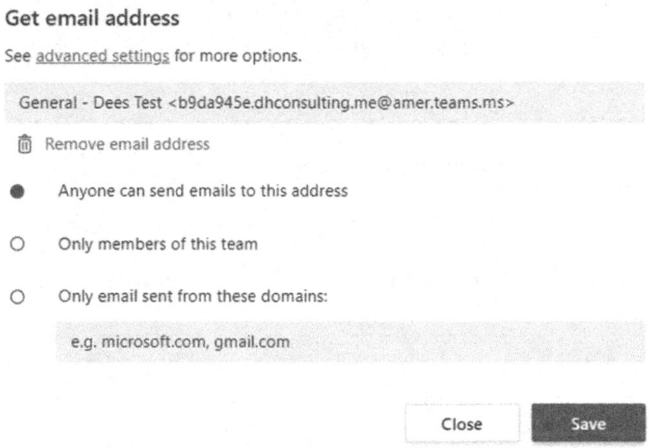

Get email address

See advanced settings for more options.

General - Dees Test <b9da945e.dhconsulting.me@amer.teams.ms>

🗑 Remove email address

● Anyone can send emails to this address

○ Only members of this team

○ Only email sent from these domains:

e.g. microsoft.com, gmail.com

[Close] [Save]

Figure 6-15. *Channel email settings*

Team and Channel Mentions

Both teams and channels can be mentioned in conversations, as seen in Figure 6-16. The main point of mentions is that they kick off notifications. A mention of a team sends notifications to everyone on the team. A mention of a channel sends notifications to everyone that follows the channel.

▾ **@mentions**   Choose who can use @team and @channel mentions

Allow @team or @[team name] mentions (this will send a notification to everyone on the team) ☑

Allow @channel or @[channel name] mentions (this will send a notification to everyone who has favorited the channel being mentioned) ☑

Figure 6-16. *@mentions*

A common complaint about Teams is that there are too many notifications, and so people stop paying attention to them. A team owner may want to disable team and channel mentions if team members are overwhelmed with notifications.

Using Tags in Teams

Tags allow you to reach a group of people at the same time. Common tags can be based on a role, skill set, a type of training, or a location. An example of a tag could be "Designer" or "Manager." Once a tag has been added, you can then @mention that tag to reach that group of people vs. individually mentioning them.

Create a Tag:

1. Navigate to the Team you want to add tags to.

2. Select the (...) for more options, and select **Manage tags**.

3. Type a tag name in the input box.

4. Add individual people to associate them to the tag.

5. Click **Create** button when complete.

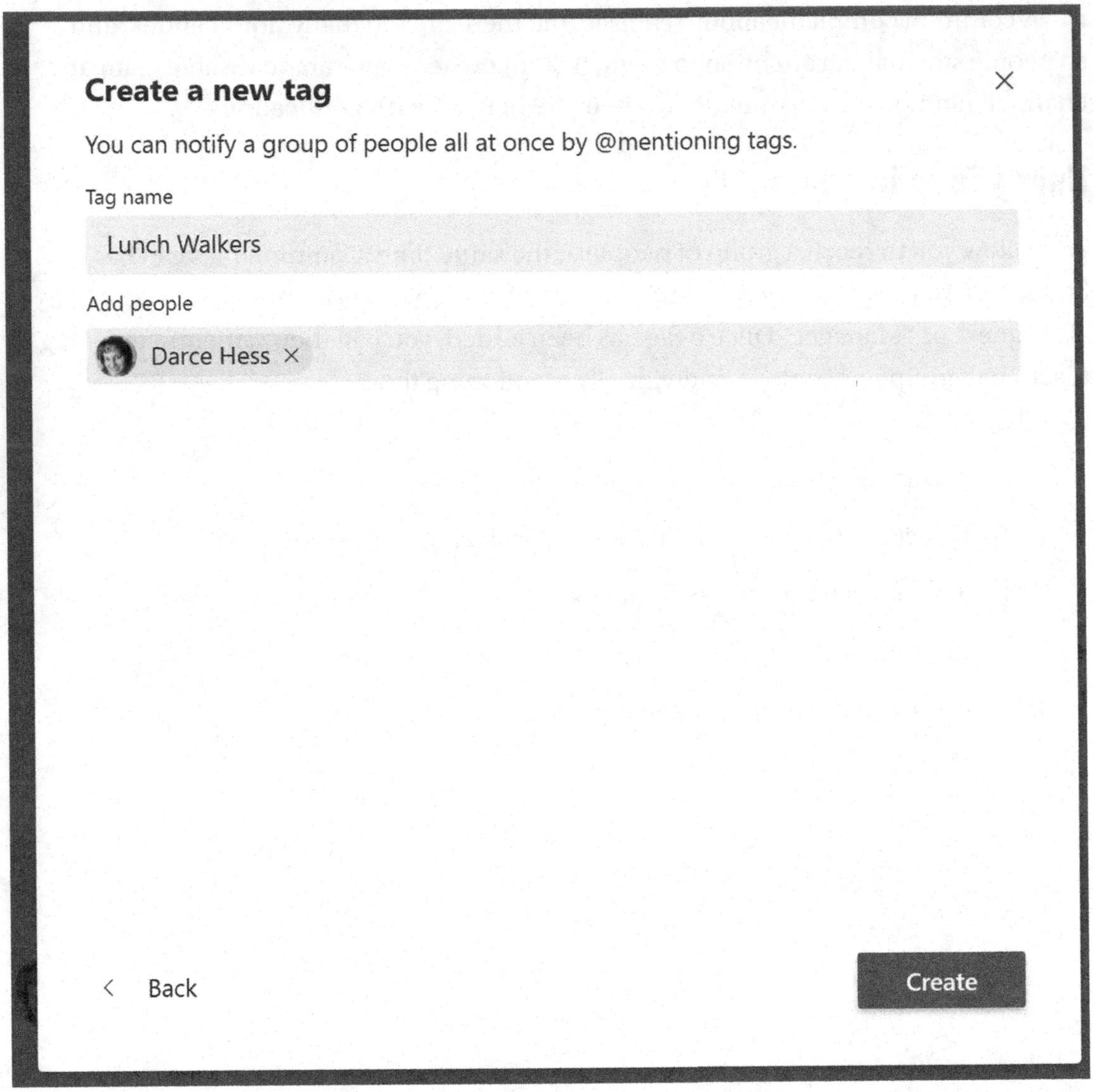

Figure 6-17. *Creating a Tag in teams*

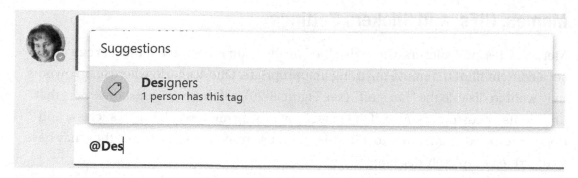

Figure 6-18. *@Mentioning a tag in a chat*

Team Templates

Team templates are prebuilt structures based around a business need or a type of project such as managing an event or working incident response. These templates can be assigned to a specific group using team policies, as seen in Figure 6-19. Team templates may also be created by a Teams Administrator to match business requirements.

Name	Description
Adopt Office 365	Help build, grow, and sustain your Champions community rollout by evangelizing and helping your peers with the new technology.
Manage a Project	Manage tasks, share documents, conduct project meetings and document risks and decisions with this template for general project management.
Manage an Event	Manage tasks, documents and collaborate on everything you need to deliver a compelling event. Invite guests users to have secure collaboration inside and outside of your company.
Onboard Employees	Improve your culture and streamline your employee onboarding with this central team for resources, questions and a bit of fun.
Organize Help Desk	Collaborate on documentation, policy and processes that support your helpdesk. Integrate your existing ticketing system or use our template to manage requests.
Collaborate on Patient Care	Streamline healthcare communication and collaboration within a ward, pod, or department. The template can be used to facilitate patient management, as well as the operational needs of a...
Collaborate on a Global Crisis or Event	Centralize collaboration for your crisis team across business units and help create business continuity plans, share remote working tips, track customer communication, and keep everyone in...
Collaborate within a Bank Branch	Centralize collaboration for your bank branch employees across Huddles, Customer Meetings, Business Processes such as Mortgage Collaboration, and keep everyone in the loop with Anno...
Coordinate Incident Response	Centralize communication and critical resources for your crisis management or incident response team. Within this team you can include many different types of files to help create a central ...
Hospital	Streamline communication and collaboration between multiple wards, pods, and departments within a hospital. This template includes a set of base channels for hospital operations, and ca...
Organize a Store	Bring your retail employees together in one central experience to manage tasks, share documents and resolve customer issues. Integrate additional applications to streamline shift start & en...

Figure 6-19. *Team templates*

Memes, GIFs, and Stickers Settings

Memes, GIFs, and stickers can be disabled by the team owner. Team owners can also set a content filter to remove anything inappropriate. One scenario where team owners may want to disable the "fun stuff" (see Figure 6-20) is if there are guest members that are clients or customers. Also, if the team is overusing memes, GIFs, and stickers, and doesn't respond to guidance to minimize their use from the team owner, they may have to resort to completely disabling them.

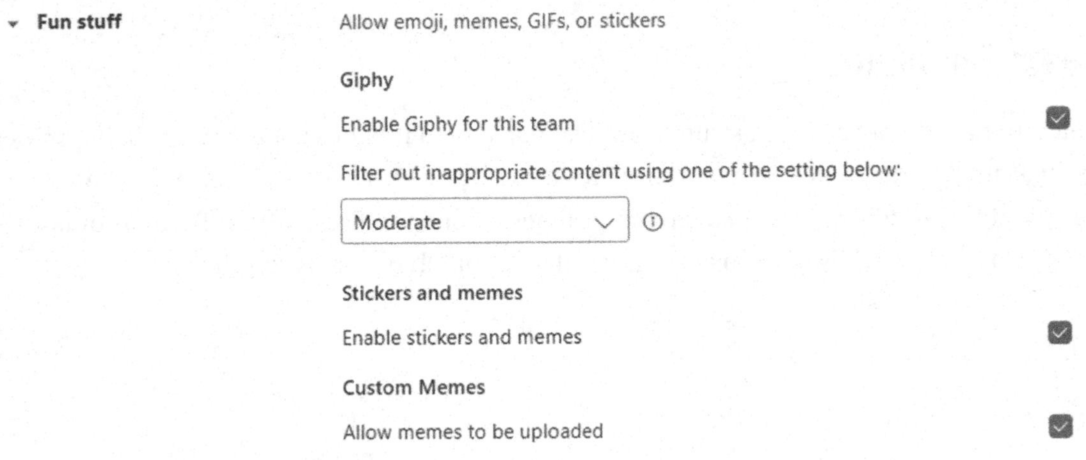

▾ **Fun stuff**	Allow emoji, memes, GIFs, or stickers	
	Giphy	
	Enable Giphy for this team	☑
	Filter out inappropriate content using one of the setting below:	
	Moderate ⌄ ⓘ	
	Stickers and memes	
	Enable stickers and memes	☑
	Custom Memes	
	Allow memes to be uploaded	☑

Figure 6-20. *Fun stuff*

Summary

In this chapter, we reviewed some of the best practices and questions you should ask when a new team is requested. As you can see, there is quite a bit to take into consideration for a proper Microsoft Teams rollout. One bright note, though, is that once you have taken the time to set this up, each corresponding team should flow easily and have a greater chance for adoption.

In the following chapter, we discuss how your organization can gain even more value from Teams by automating business processes using Power Automate and chatbots.

CHAPTER 7

Automating Business Processes in Teams

In the modern workplace, the automation of business processes and information gathering is becoming more and more commonplace. If a task at work is routine, simple, and repetitive and involves data entry or searching for information, it is likely a good candidate for business process automation. With Microsoft Teams being a digital workspace that is meant to serve as a catalyst for communication, collaboration, decision making, and creativity, it makes sense to automate as many tasks as possible so that the focus is on bringing the team to the next level of success. Microsoft Teams allows data from third-party cloud-based applications to be leveraged, so the possibilities for business process automation are vast. Business process automation can be achieved in Microsoft Teams using bots and Microsoft Flow.

What Are Bots?

Since Microsoft Teams is a chat-based application, it isn't surprising that you are able to automate some business processes by chatting with a bot. A *bot* is a program that is configured to send predefined messages and decision prompts to end users, which help them to streamline and automate processes. Microsoft Teams offers a platform for team members to interact with intelligent bots in both natural conversations in chat and through specific commands, depending on the bot installed. Bots in Microsoft Teams connect with cloud services. For the most part, bots are built to quickly run simple and repetitive tasks that would take a person much longer to complete. Bots in Microsoft Teams connect with cloud services. They are built by developers using the Microsoft Bot Framework, which allows them to easily connect with Microsoft Teams and the App Store.

© Melissa Hubbard, Matthew J. Bailey, D'arce Hess, Mårten Hellebro 2021
M. Hubbard et al., *Mastering Microsoft Teams*, https://doi.org/10.1007/978-1-4842-6898-8_7

In Microsoft Teams, bots are initiated in chat messages or in conversation messages in channels; but depending on the bot installed, it may only work in one or the other. When you send a bot a message, it usually sends instructions on what functionality it has to offer. Figure 7-1 shows examples of the bots available in Teams. Some of the apps have other components, such as a tool that can be used in a tab.

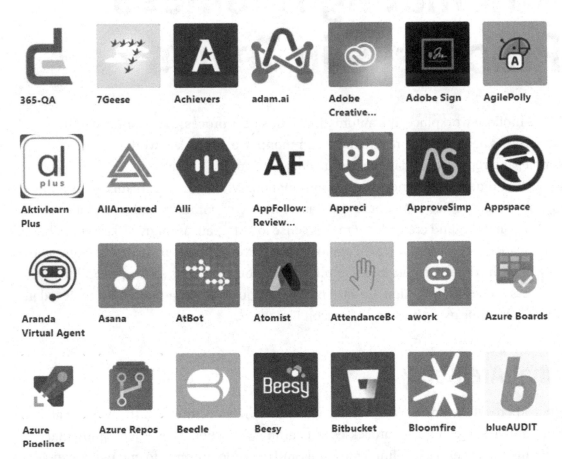

Figure 7-1. Examples of apps with bots available in Teams

Note   The list of bots available in Microsoft Teams is constantly changing as new bots are developed.

What Bots Can Do

Microsoft Teams comes with many options for bots that help team members with a variety of business processes. One such example is the bot "Polly." One option available with Polly is to check in with new Team members how their first 30 days on the job are going.

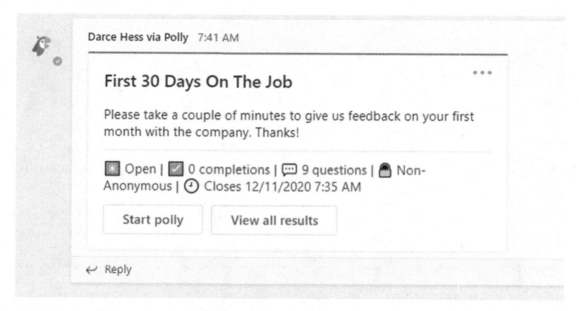

Figure 7-2. *Example of Polly Bot*

Bots in Microsoft Teams connect users with cloud services and then leverage that cloud service's functionality to perform basic jobs in Teams when you chat with them and give them commands. Bots help Microsoft Teams users with job duties such as scheduling meetings or events, taking polls to gather information from team members, and managing team tasks. In some cases, you may find one bot that does everything you need to automate your business process. Otherwise, it may be necessary to install and combine the functionality of two or more bots. Although apps in the Microsoft Teams store are organized into the categories of Analytics and BI, Developer and IT, Education, Human Resources, Productivity, Project Management, Sales and Support, and Social and Fun, the three main functions that bots are performing are scheduling, task management, and polling. Figure 7-3 shows how apps are organized in the Microsoft Teams App Store.

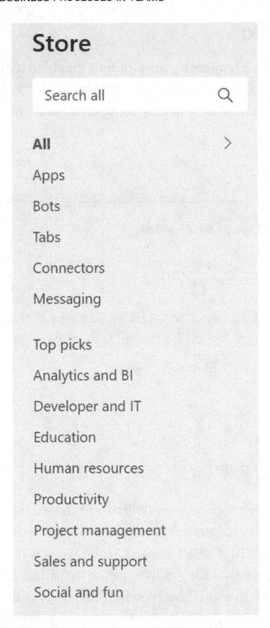

Figure 7-3. *Organization of apps in the Microsoft Teams App Store*

Scheduling

Scheduling meetings can be a time-consuming task that bots in Teams can assist with. Some examples of how bots can organize meetings are by syncing calendars of team members and showing available times to pick from, polling attendees to vote on the best meeting time, scheduling a meeting and sending out meeting invites, and even providing a list of meeting rooms to book based on which are available.

Although we know meetings can be held in Teams, some organizations that use other products for meetings can disable this feature. Many common meetings services have bots in Teams, so when using the bot, team members are able to create meetings within these services.

Task Management

Bots in Microsoft Teams can assist project managers with tasks such as collecting daily status reports from team members. Reminders to complete status reports can be automatically sent by a bot, and then team members can respond with their status, which is added to a report that can be viewed by the project manager. Reminders to team members can be configured based on when they are due.

There are also bots that can track and manage documents and tasks through their life cycles. Task-based time tracking is also possible within Microsoft Teams using a bot. Project management business processes that involve collecting information, tracking, and reminders can be automated with bots.

Polling

There are bots in Microsoft Teams that have polling capabilities. Polling is a simple way to get feedback from team members by providing them a predefined list of choices that they can select from. Team members can be automatically notified in Microsoft Teams when there is a new poll. The bot consolidates the responses, allowing for the results to be analyzed. Although this functionality may seem trivial, it can be extremely powerful and a huge time saver when trying to seek the opinions of team members when making a decision.

How to Add Bots

Bots can be added to a team by every team member unless the setting is changed by either the Office 365 administrator or the team owner, as shown in Figure 7-4.

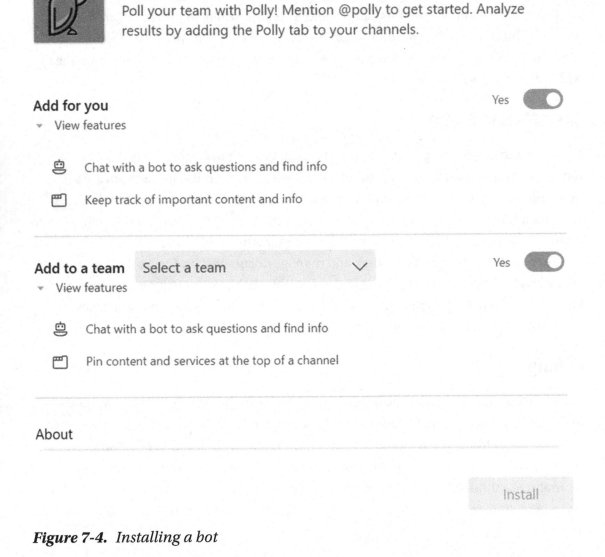

Figure 7-4. *Installing a bot*

Note   External apps can be disabled by the Office 365 administrator. If you cannot add a bot, this could be the issue.

To add a bot to a team

1. Click the ellipse (…) to the right of the team that you want to add the bot to.

2. Click **Manage team**.

3. Click **Apps**.

4. Click the **Go to Store** button.

5. Click **bots** on the left underneath Store to show only the bot apps.

6. Select the bot to add to the team.

7. Select the team name from the **Add to team** drop-down menu, and then click **Install**.

Using Power Automate with Teams

Power Automate is a cloud-based application that is part of Office 365 and can be used for free as part of the same subscription with Microsoft Teams. Power Automate is a business process automation tool that can collect data, automate approvals, copy files, send notifications, and more. Power Automate can connect data from Microsoft Teams with data from other Office 365 applications, as well as third-party cloud-based applications.

For a flow to run, it needs to be triggered. There are many triggers that stem from hundreds of applications, but some examples are when an item in SharePoint is created or modified, when a new Microsoft Forms response is submitted, or when an Office 365 Outlook event is added, updated, or deleted. There are currently triggers for when channel messages are added, for a select message, when a new team member is added, and when I am mentioned in a channel. Once a flow is triggered, conditions can be added that allow for different things to happen based on if they are true or not. Actions are tasks that the flow performs. Actions are what the flow does to complete the business process.

Teams Actions in Power Automate

There are four actions that Power Automate performs in Microsoft Teams, as shown in Figure 7-5. These actions provide an automatic way to create a channel, list the channels, list teams, and post messages.

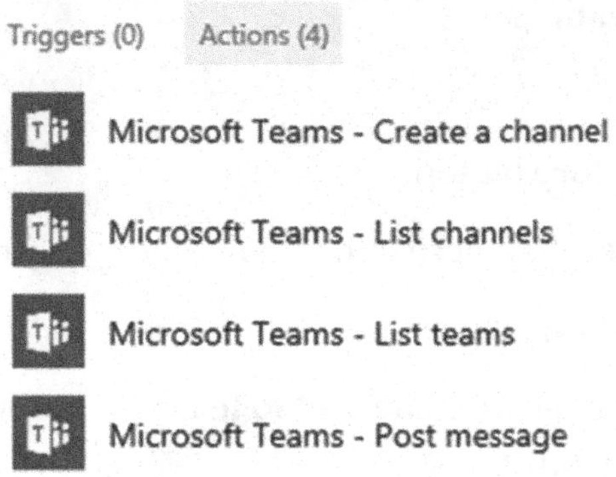

Triggers (0)   Actions (4)

T|| Microsoft Teams - Create a channel

T|| Microsoft Teams - List channels

T|| Microsoft Teams - List teams

T|| Microsoft Teams - Post message

Figure 7-5. *Teams actions available in Microsoft Flow*

Create a Channel

The *Create a channel* action in Microsoft Teams (see Figure 7-6) is extremely useful. This action automatically creates a channel based on a trigger. An attribute from a previous step can be used as the channel name; for example, you can create a flow that is triggered when an item is added to a SharePoint list. It then performs the action of creating a channel using the Title field from the SharePoint item as the channel name. A step can be added to the flow to only allow the creation of a channel if someone in authority approves, such as the team owner or an IT professional.

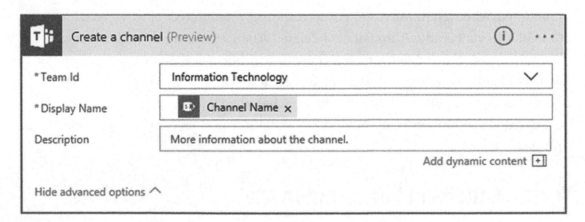

Figure 7-6. *Creating a channel action in Power Automate*

List Channels

The *List channels* action (see Figure 7-7) automatically provides a list of the channels in a team. It monitors channel creation; for example, an IT department could receive a weekly list of all channels to make sure that there aren't channels being created inappropriately. A condition can be added to the flow to only list channels that were created within a certain amount of days.

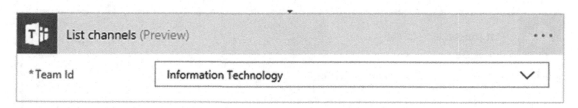

Figure 7-7. *List channels actions in Power Automate*

List Teams

The *List teams* action (see Figure 7-8) is similar to the list channels action, except the teams are listed, not the channels. This is a great way to automate the process of monitoring the teams created in an Office 365 tenant. The team name, team ID, and team description attributes can be listed in an email or a report. Only the teams that the user running the flow is part of are listed.

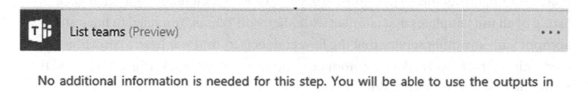

Figure 7-8. *List teams action in Power Automate*

Post Message

The *Post message* action (see Figure 7-9) is likely the most commonly used Microsoft Teams action in Microsoft Flow. It notifies a team when something of interest has happened outside of Microsoft Teams. Common scenarios are to post a message to a team channel when a task in SharePoint is marked complete, when a new form is submitted, or when a bug is opened in Visual Studio Team Services.

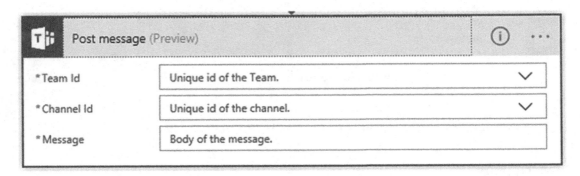

Figure 7-9. *Post message action in Microsoft Flow*

Templates

Power Automate offers several prebuilt templates. There is very little configuration involved when using templates, and they are the easiest way to get started with using Power Automate. As shown in Figure 7-10, you can search for teams, and then get a listing of all the templates that connect with Microsoft Teams. You need to have an account with any other service that the flow connects to, and you have to provide credentials for it to work. Power Automate templates can act as a starting point, and then steps and conditions can be added.

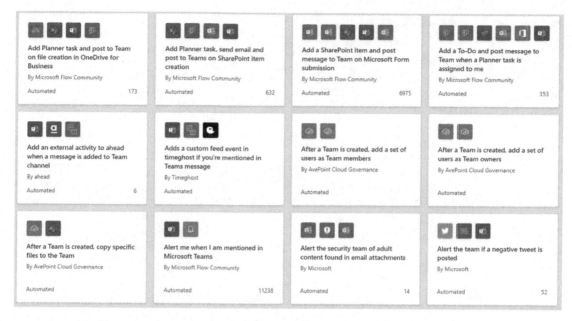

Figure 7-10. *Team templates in Power Automate*

Power Automate App in Teams

The Microsoft Flow app, which can be installed in Microsoft Teams, provides a chat bot. This personal app helps users keep track of their flows. Flows can be created and edited within Teams. Since the Microsoft Flow app is a personal app, it is not seen by other team members. Each user installs the Microsoft Flow app themselves and can display their flows and approvals.

With the Microsoft Flow bot in Teams (see Figure 7-11), flows are run by command. When you chat with the Microsoft Flow bot, it lists the available flows to run. You can then command it to run a flow by typing **Run flow** followed by the number listed for the particular flow. At this time, only flows that run on a schedule are initiated by the Microsoft Flow bot. If you create a scheduled flow that lists all channels in a team and sends them in a monthly report, you can use the Microsoft Flow bot to send the report on demand as needed in Teams. Another scenario is if you have a scheduled flow that regularly posts articles, website links, or messages to social media sites such as LinkedIn or Twitter, you can use the Microsoft Flow bot to post on demand.

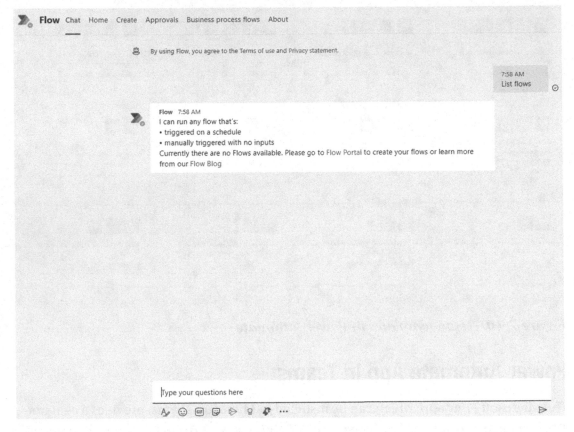

Figure 7-11. *Flow bot in Teams*

Using Power Apps with Teams

Power Apps allow users to create easy no-code and low-code apps that can help to track business processes such as tracking time-off requests, submitting expenses, and gathering ideas. These apps can be created in as little as five minutes and can provide a tremendous amount of value.

Power Apps will get added as a tab within a specified channel.

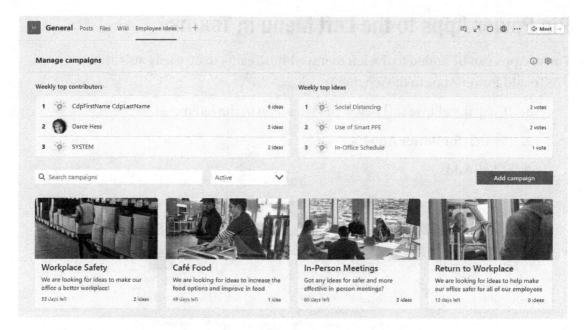

Figure 7-12. Employee Ideas Power App within Teams

Each Power App may have their own permissions and settings. When adding a Power App, be sure to check what the default settings are for the app and who is allowed to use it.

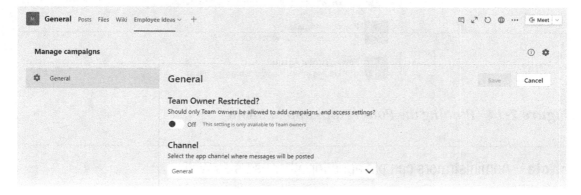

Figure 7-13. Employee Ideas Power App settings within Teams - General Settings

Pin Power Apps to the Left Menu in Teams

Power Apps can be added to the left menu within Teams to be easily accessible.

To add Power Apps to the left menu

1. Click the ellipse (...) below the Files icon in the left menu.

2. Search for **Power Apps**.

3. Click **Add**.

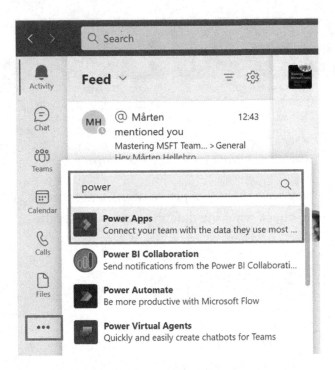

Figure 7-14. *Pinning the Power Apps app in Menu*

Note   Administrators can pin apps for other users as well.

Summary

In this chapter, we reviewed the ways you can automate your business processes in Microsoft Teams using bots, Power Apps, and Power Automate. There are many benefits and timesaving opportunities with automating business processes in Microsoft Teams, but this is a more advanced aspect of the product that isn't always necessary. Focusing on users adopting the basic Microsoft Teams functionality is much more important. Be advised that although bots and flows are fairly new and exciting, they should not be set up if there is no business need. However, if you or a team member is spending a lot of time on an arduous task that is simple and repetitive, it is definitely worth exploring the business process automation options available within Microsoft Teams.

CHAPTER 8

Known Challenges and the Future

Microsoft Teams is constantly adding new features and functionality. Like any application, you will possibly find some challenges with Microsoft Teams when you use it. Although Microsoft Teams does a lot to boost collaboration and comunication, you may also find some challenges in trying to accomplish your tasks as you work with it daily. This might sound a bit discouraging, but Microsoft *is* investing in Microsoft Teams a great deal—more so than some of its other software. Depending on when you are reading this book (compared to when it was written), knowing the road map, issues, and user feedback can help make a realistic plan on how to use Microsoft Teams. In this chapter, we discuss issues that may occur when using Microsoft Teams.

Microsoft Teams replaces Skype for Business Online in Office 365 during 2021 (it is not replacing Skype for Business On-Premises at the time of writing this book). Microsoft Teams has most of the Skype for Business Online features but has added lots of new functionality that Skype users could never have dreamed of.

Microsoft Teams is a new generation of collaboration software, in which the ability to work with others on files and conversations is provided. When you put these all together, you see that there are a myriad of different features coming to Microsoft Teams.

Remember, Microsoft Teams is changing at a rapid pace, and depending on when you are reading this book, *some of the issues discussed in this chapter may have been fixed or have had work-arounds.*

Challenges with Working in Teams

In this section, we review some of the issues you might encounter while completing your work in Microsoft Teams.

© Melissa Hubbard, Matthew J. Bailey, D'arce Hess, Mårten Hellebro 2021
M. Hubbard et al., *Mastering Microsoft Teams*, https://doi.org/10.1007/978-1-4842-6898-8_8

Editing Office Documents

Let's say that you are writing a book and that you are consistently typing long paragraphs and pasting images into a Word document. The flow of how you work depends on how you created the Word document. As you can see in Figure 8-1, there are different ways to get a document in Teams.

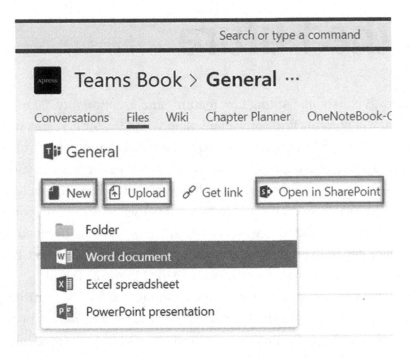

Figure 8-1. *The many ways to create or upload a document in Teams*

Microsoft has made a good deal of effort to create a seamless experience for users, so that working with Office files appears to be similar, regardless of how you access or create them. However, there are some features that differ among methods. An example of this is when you create a Microsoft Teams Word document in a browser. This is really just embedding a Word Online authoring experience inside Microsoft Teams. Some people may not realize this. With Word Online, there is no ability to change the autosave timing. Word Online saves data as you type it. However, with the installed version of Word, you have the full set of Word configuration options.

The challenge is that creating a unified interface has good points and not-so-good points. If you are creating Word documents that are not very large, the online Word experience typically works well. For large documents, however, it is better to use the Word client by either opening the document in Word from Microsoft Teams or by creating a new file in Word and later uploading it to the files tab.

Importing and Exporting Channels, Data, and Files

A limitation of Microsoft Teams is its ability to move some of its data between channels and/or other teams. Microsoft Teams has added the ability to move files but it is currently unable to move conversations or posts in a channel. If you plan properly, you can avoid a lot of issues involving the need to move the data around. However, as we explain in an upcoming section, the inability to secure channels differently from the team itself will cause people to organize them in different ways. This means that if you need to change how the team is organized and who sees what, you will not be able to move data and conversations to a new place. Because Microsoft does not make public all the plans for its software, it is unknown if the company is working on a tool to move these items.

Having Channel-Only Members

Many organizations work in different ways. In some cases, you may only want to invite someone to a specific channel to join a conversation without having them be a member of an entire team. This would also be a scenario in which you were working with outside contractors or guest users. Having the permissions be at the Team level allows those members to see all of the information for the entire Team with the exception of a private channel. The good news is that Microsoft currently has this on the backlog, and we will hopefully see this come to life in the near future.

Public Channels

There are a couple of reasons that having a public channel would be useful or larger organizations. With a public team, any member of the organization would be able to join a single channel of a Team vs. needing to join the entire team. An additional reason is that in the current architecture, many companies will end up creating both a public team and a private team—one for the department to collaborate internally with and one for the rest of the organization to collaborate with the department. This causes two places where someone may need to go to work with that team and two places for a member of that department to have to follow up on conversations. By having a public channel within a private team, it would allow for the department members to have a place to collaborate or receive feedback from the larger organization without having to maintain two separate teams.

Converting Private Channels to Public Channels

Teams has gained a lot of adoption by the ease of use. When private channels were introduced, it fulfilled a major gap for many organizations. However, a result of this is that many users created private channels for conversation between a smaller group of users and then realized that the conversation needed to be opened up to a larger audience or no longer needed to be private. Today, you are unable to change the status of a private channel to be public. The only way, today, would be to create a new public channel and try to copy and paste the conversations into the new channel. This isn't a great experience. We are optimistic that we will see the ability to convert between private channels and public channels coming in the future.

Read-Only Permissions

There are at least two reasons for having a read-only team, and one of them has been delivered just as this book was going to press. The first is for archival purposes. This *archive* option is now available in the "gear" icon at the bottom left of your Microsoft Teams interface.

The second reason, which is still unavailable when this book was being published, is to create an information-only team where users can only read information and only managers can post information. Although you can change member permissions in team settings to only allow owners to post messages, this isn't exactly the same as a read-only team that is still in an active status.

Duplicate Team Names

One issue that could be confusing to your users is that Teams allows you to create teams with the same name, as seen in Figure 8-2. On the back end, the team is really a unique number called a GUID (globally unique identifier). The system uses this GUID to manage the team behind the scenes, so the duplicate name issue is not relevant to the system. The *display name* is what users see. As shown in Figure 8-2, multiple teams with the same name can confuse users who do not know which team is which.

Figure 8-2. *Teams with the same display name can be created*

Have an IT administrator or programmer create a script to prevent duplicate names, or purchase Azure Premium to take advantage of the groups naming policy feature to work around this issue.

Deleting a Team Without Deleting the Group

When creating a new team, you have the option to use an existing Office 365 group, as shown in Figure 8-3. This is beneficial if your group members are certain that they want to use Teams as a replacement for Office 365 Groups. However, if users change their mind and decide they would like to go back to only using the original Office 365 group, there is an important issue. There is no way to disembark a group from a team. This means that if you delete the team, you also delete the pre-existing group with it.

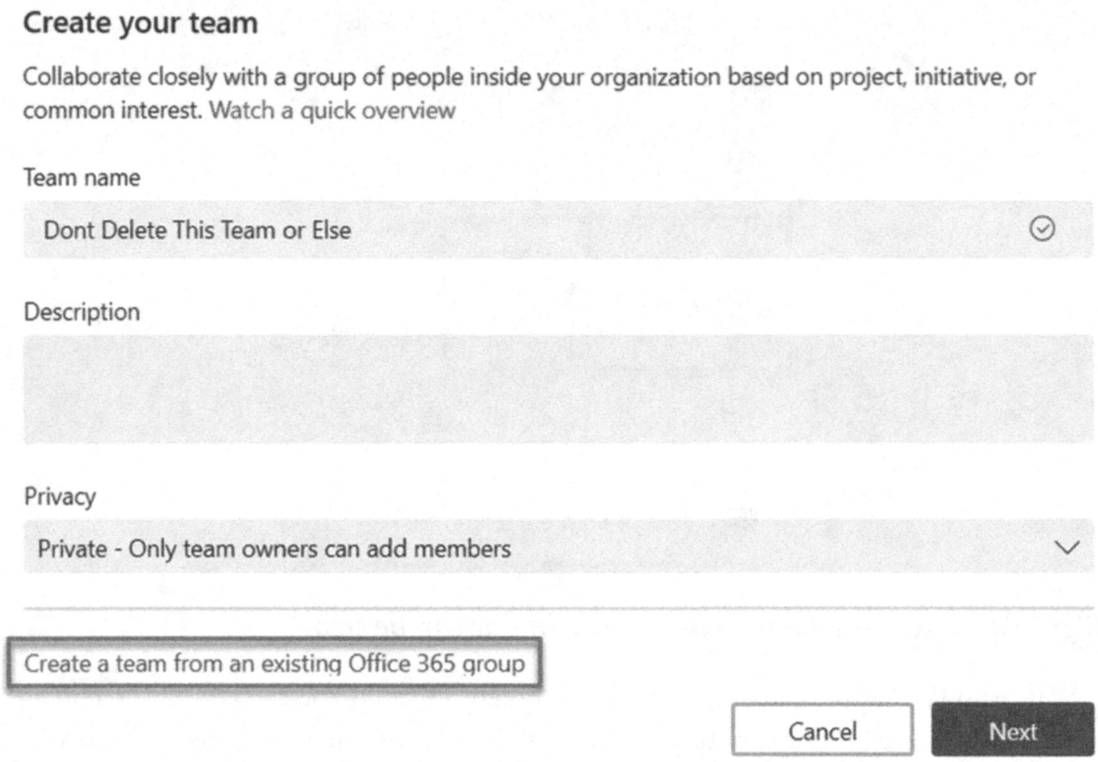

Create your team

Collaborate closely with a group of people inside your organization based on project, initiative, or common interest. Watch a quick overview

Team name

Dont Delete This Team or Else   ⊘

Description

Privacy

Private - Only team owners can add members   ⌄

Create a team from an existing Office 365 group

Cancel   Next

Figure 8-3. *The option to create a team from an existing Office 365 group*

Caution   There is no way to detach a group from a team at this time. Be certain that you want to convert your existing groups to teams.

Teams Can Have Performance Issues

When Microsoft Teams users lack solid Internet connection or it is not confgured properly, performance issues can occur. Depending on what you are doing in Microsoft Teams, the amount of resources the Teams client uses can vary. It is important to note that Teams runs multiple processes at the same time. If you think about it, Teams is somewhat like trying to run Skype for Business, OneDrive for Business, Outlook, and any other application connected to it at the same time. At times is can use quite a bit of your computer's resources. Microsoft is always working on performance improvements, and has provided guidance for how to best prepare your network for Teams.

Challenges with Communicating in Teams

Now let's move on to some of the challenges you may face while communicating in Microsoft Teams.

Channel Email Addresses

As discussed earlier in the book, a channel comes with an email address to send to. This is great for making sure that an email is kept with the team and not a user's email box. If others are going to use this email address on a longer-term basis, the need for a simple and memorable email address might be of value. An example of an automatically created email address is seen in Figure 8-4. Unfortunately, the channel email address cannot be changed.

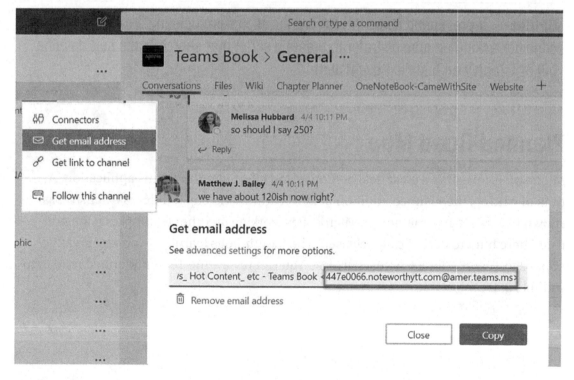

Figure 8-4. A channel email address is pre-created by Teams for you

Issues with Governing Teams

In this section, we review some known issues with governing Microsoft Teams.

Team Deletion

There is no way to prevent an owner from deleting their own team. This may or may not be a concern in your organization. As an alternative solution, as an Office 365 administrator, you can monitor teams being deleted. The administrator can place an alert in the Security & Compliance Center to send an email to a specific person if a team is deleted. The team is recoverable for 30 days after the date that it was deleted. Unfortunately, if you are an end user, you most likely do not have permission to the Office 365 admin center. You will need to ask for your team to be restored.

Caution   If preventing users in your organization from deleting a team is needed, consider asking an administrator to create a script that searches the soft deletion bin or to apply an audit log event alert.

Planned Road Map

Microsoft is investing a great deal of money and effort into the Teams application. At time of writing, the planned addition of new features and capabilities is extensive, as shown in Table 8-1. Additionally, Microsoft is working on other features that are not listed here but are periodically released. The "continuous learning" concept greatly applies to Teams—for a few years at least. You can review the Teams' planned road map in Table 8-1.

Table 8-1. *Teams Features Expected to Be Released in 2018 by Microsoft (Estimates, Not Guarantees)*

Feature	Early to Mid-2021	End-of-Year 2021
Tasks publishing and reporting for firstline workers	X	
Updated functionality for downloading participant reports in Teams meetings	X	
View all upcoming assignments in the Teams calendar	X	
SharePoint home site app	X	
Meeting attendee registration	X	
Live reactions	X	
Support for Cortana voice assistance on Microsoft Teams Room devices	X	
Live Transcription with speaker attribution	X	
Data loss prevention for Microsoft Teams in GCC High and DoD	X	
Include computer sound when sharing a Desktop or Window on Mac for worldwide multi-tenant and GCC	X	
Meeting chat moderation settings	X	
Microsoft Teams panels	X	
Support for breakout rooms for Microsoft Teams Rooms on Android	X	
Personal productivity insights in Teams	X	
Personal well-being insights in Teams	X	
Collaborative calling	X	
Updated layouts for meetings on Android	X	
Increasing Chat Size from 300 to 1000 participants	X	
Better together for calls on Teams phones	X	

User Feedback

A fair number of new features have come from user feedback on the UserVoice website at `https://microsoftteams.uservoice.com/forums/555103-public` (see Figure 8-5). Microsoft actively monitors user requests and responds on the site. Some requests are accepted, some are declined, some are investigated, and some are put on the backlog. Although there is no guarantee that a request will be addressed, the more popular ones seem to receive some type of notation. In any case, take a look at the UserVoice website; you can voice your opinion or vote on an idea that is important to you.

Note   As of time of this publication, Microsoft has announced they will start moving away from UserVoice over time and focus on more of a directional feedback approach. Some of this will include allowing users to submit feedback directly in the Teams product which can also be viewed by the tenant administrator. This feature must be enabled in your tenant for it to be available.

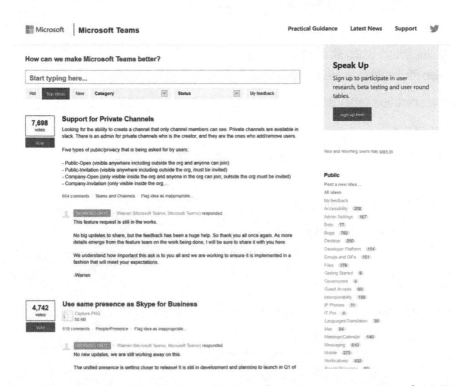

Figure 8-5. *Showing the UserVoice website, where new suggestions for Microsoft Teams are tracked between product users and Microsoft employees*

Summary

We have covered existing issues, user frustrations, and planned updates for Microsoft Teams in this chapter. Additionally, we provided an extensive end user guide to practical usage, collaboration, and governance within Microsoft Teams.

Microsoft Teams is one of the first applications that Microsoft released with the concept of an agile, continuous delivery concept. This means that we all have to keep our eyes open when using Microsoft Teams, as it will change often. By deciding to use Microsoft Teams, you have taken a step in the right direction toward transforming collaboration and communication with your teammates.

CHAPTER 9

Teams for Education

Using technology as a way to improve our capabilities to teach children and help educators continues to be a priority. With the increase in the numbers of schools and programs that are required to implement remote learning initiatives, Teams provides a way to help bridge the gap between in-person classrooms and the virtual classrooms of our current time. With a focus on tools that are only available for those with a Microsoft Education tenant, Teams has become the perfect partner for those wanting to expand their reach and continue to engage and communicate with students, faculty, and staff.

This chapter discusses how to create Teams for education as well as how to work with assignments, grades, and other resources that can help every child and teacher be ready for their classes in no time.

Getting Started

When you first open Teams, you may also ready have a few classes that have been provisioned for you. The default view for your teams is in a card-like format. If you find this distracting, or would like to see more about your teams, you can switch the view to be a list format that is the layout from earlier chapters in this book.

© Melissa Hubbard, Matthew J. Bailey, D'arce Hess, Mårten Hellebro 2021
M. Hubbard et al., *Mastering Microsoft Teams*, https://doi.org/10.1007/978-1-4842-6898-8_9

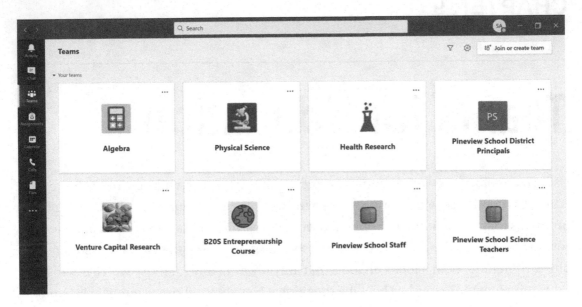

Figure 9-1. *Default Teams view for education*

To switch the view

1.   Click the settings (gear) icon in the upper-left corner.

2.   Select **Switch View**.

3.   Under **Layout**, select **List**.

You will now see all of your teams vertically in the left column. You can always switch the views back by going back to the settings and selecting **Grid**.

Available Team Templates

Microsoft provides several different options for the type of Teams that you can create. The type will be determined by who you want to be a member and also the topic of focus that you would like to use it for. There are four templates available to help you get started: Class, Professional Learning Community, Staff, and Other. We will go into a bit more about what each of these templates offers and when it is best to use them in the following.

Class Template

Class templates are perfect for the traditional classroom experience. They are great for classroom discussions, group projects, and assignments. In a class template, the teachers are automatically made as the default team owners, and students are added as members of the team.

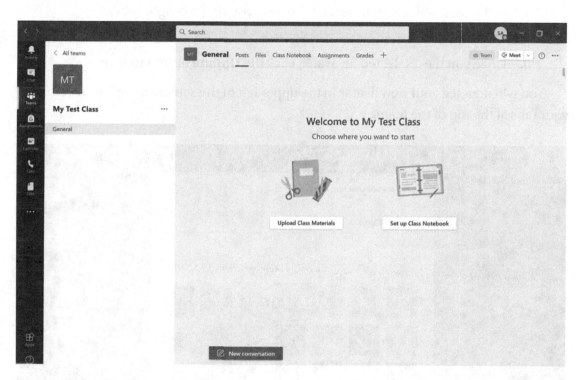

Figure 9-2. *The contents of the class template when used*

Selecting a Class Avatar

For every team and class, you can select a custom icon to be used as an avatar for that class. You can also choose to upload your own. Microsoft provides a wide range of icons to help you get started. Using an avatar can help to make identifying the class easier for students and teachers when working with multiple classes.

To add a logo

1. Select the logo square in the upper-left corner of your class or team.

2. Use the drop-down menu to select what grade level your class is for and a category of class such as "Arts and Music." The avatars will filter based on your selection to help you find the right avatar for your class.

3. Once you have selected an avatar, click the **Update** button to save.

You will now see your new avatar in the upper left of the screen as well as next to your tabs at the top of the team.

Figure 9-3. *Creating a team using the class template*

Working with Class Materials

Class materials are any type of documents that you want to share with students. Students will have read-only permissions to the documents in this library. Only teachers have the ability to edit the documents. You can add the documents through the Teams' interface by clicking the files tab located at the top of the team. As with all places that contain documents in Teams, the class materials actually live within a SharePoint document library and can be accessed using the "Open in SharePoint" option to be able to view additional information about the document.

Figure 9-4. *Class materials*

Setting Up a Class Notebook

The class notebook uses Microsoft OneNote to create four primary areas:

- Collaboration Space – A place where team notes are stored and everyone has the ability to see them. Both teachers and students can edit the content in the collaboration space.

- Content Library – An area where course materials can be stored. Teachers have the ability to edit the content, and students will have read-only access.

- Teacher-Only Section – This area is available only for teachers. Notes and content can be stored here. Students will not be able to view the content in this section.

- Student Notebooks – Each student will be given a place where they can gain notes from teachers. This area is private to each student, and they cannot view other students' notebooks. The teacher will have edit permissions in this notebook.

In each student's notebook, the teacher can set up the sections that will appear for that student. Example sections you may want to consider would be Handouts, Class Notes, Homework, or Quizzes to get you started. You can add additional sections based on the needs of your class.

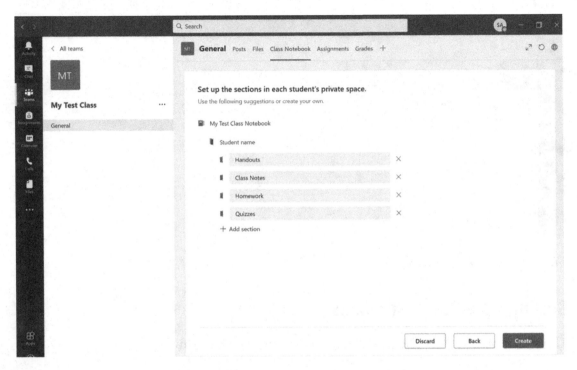

Figure 9-5. *Student notebook setup*

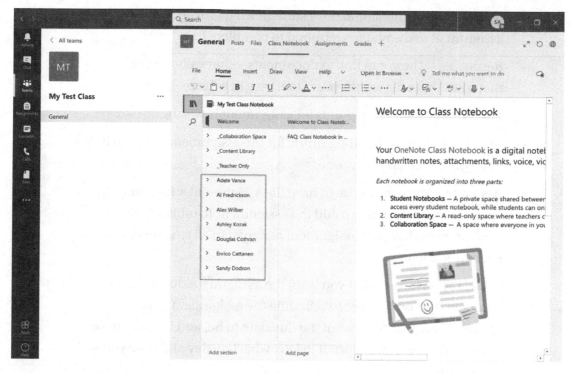

Figure 9-6. *Individual student notebooks*

Working with Assignments

Assignments that can be given to students can range in topics and complexity based on the needs of the class and the subject. New assignments can be created based on a previous assignment or from scratch. You also have the option to create quizzes and rubrics for grading.

Creating an Assignment

You can reach the assignments through two ways. The first is by clicking the "Assignments" icon in the left navigation; within your class, click the **Assignments** tab at the top of your team. When you create your first assignment, you will be prompted for several fields to fill in:

- Title – This should be the name of the assignment.

- Category – Can be tied to a topic such as "Book Reports" or "Discussion Post."

- Instructions – This should tell a student what is expected of the assignment and any steps required to complete it.

- Resources – These can link to documents, other websites, or materials that exist within your OneDrive or a Team.

- Points – The number of points an assignment is worth.

- Rubric – If there is a grading rubric for the assignment, you can link to it or you can create a new one.

- Assign to – You can choose to have the assignment added to the class that you are in, or you can add the assignment to other classes. You can choose to have the assignment assigned to all students or to specific students.

- Date Due – The date that you want the assignment due from the students. You can choose to schedule the assignment to post on a specific date, when you want the due date to be, and if you choose to allow for students to turn it in late, what late day and time you will allow up to.

- Settings – If you have multiple channels for a class, you can select which channel you want the notifications posted to.

After you post the assignment, a notification will be sent out within the channel letting students know that a new assignment has posted. The message will also appear in the Activity feed from the left menu.

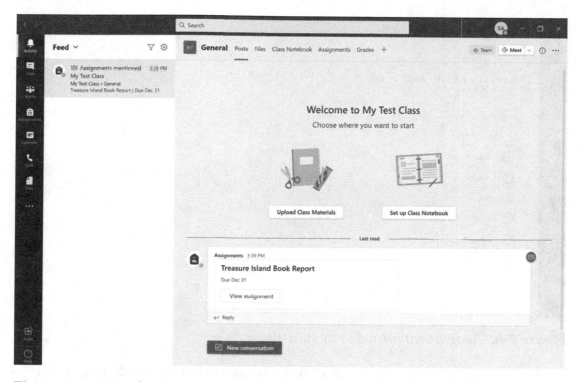

Figure 9-7. *Posted assignment in Channel*

Grading an Assignment

You will be able to view which of your students has turned in an assignment by navigating back to the Assignments tab and selecting the assignment that you would like to view. When you open the assignment, you will see the list of names of students that are associated to that class. To the side of each student, you will see a notification if the student turned in the assignment. If you have a longer list of students, you can also choose to search for a specific student from the search box.

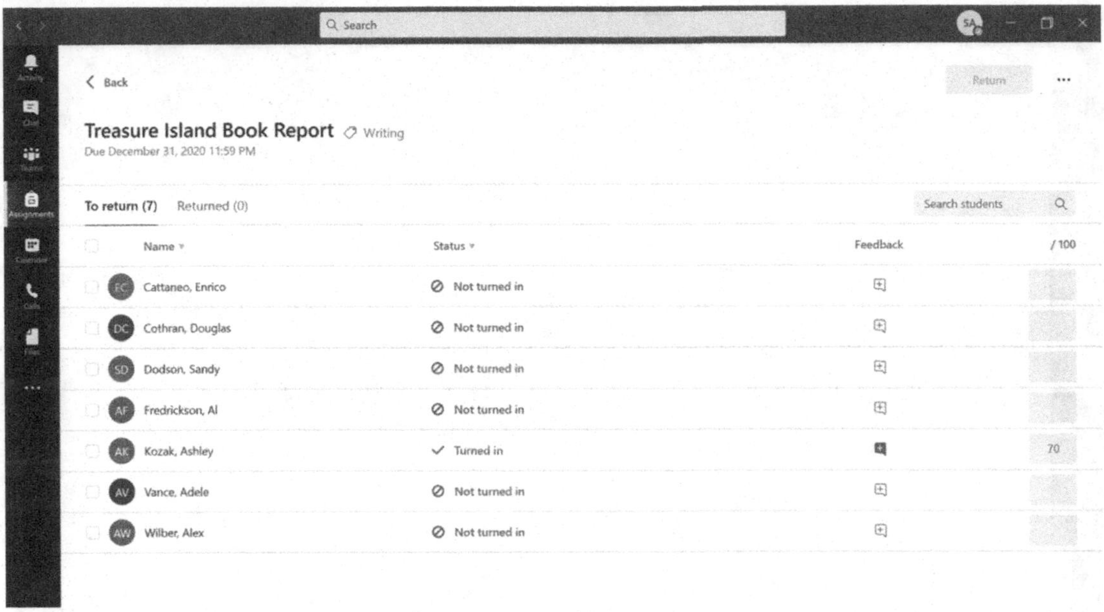

Figure 9-8. *Assignment turned in by students*

To view and grade the assignment, click the **Turned in** button. It will bring up the assignment with a pane on the right side to be able to provide feedback as you grade the assignment as well as provide a specific point value. If you have used a grading rubric, you can click specific selections within the rubric and provide feedback for the grading.

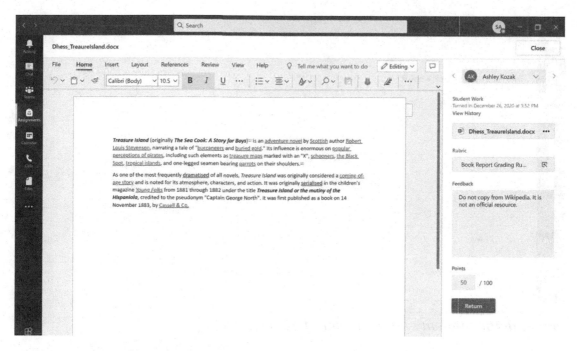

Figure 9-9. *Grading an assignment*

Note   Clicking Return does not return just a grade, it returns the assignment to the student to improve on, and they can resubmit. If no adjustments need to be made, close the view in the upper-right corner.

Hiding the Student's Names from Assignments

In some cases, you may want to grade solely based on the quality of the work without knowing the individual student's name that turned it in. This can help with unconscious bias during grading.

Let's review how to remove student's names when grading assignments.

1. Make sure you are within the assignment view.

2. Click the ellipse (…) in the upper-right corner of the screen.

3. Select **Hide student names** from the drop-down menu.

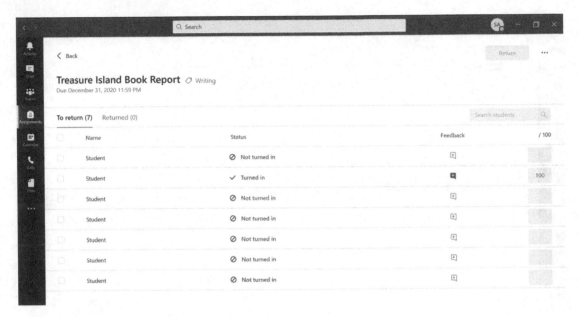

Figure 9-10. *Student's names removed from view*

Working with Quizzes

Quizzes are often created to help test the knowledge students have learned about a topic or lesson. Microsoft utilizes an application called "Forms" to create quizzes for classes. Forms may also be used to create surveys as well as quizzes to gain feedback from students on a topic.

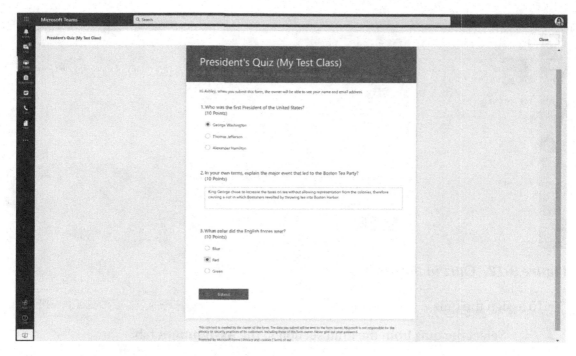

Figure 9-11. *Student's view of a quiz*

Create a Quiz

To create a quiz, you will follow the same initial steps as creating an assignment:

1. Make sure you are within the Assignments tab in your class.

2. Click the **Create** button.

3. Select **Quiz** from the drop-down menu.

Once Forms opens, you can select the type of answer for a question such as choice, long answer, or a rating. Once finished with the creation of your quiz, simply exit out of forms. Your quiz will be saved as a draft assignment.

Assigning a Quiz

You can find all quizzes that have not been assigned within the "Assignments" tab in the Draft area.

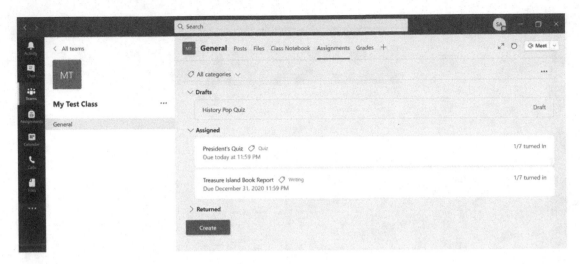

Figure 9-12. *Quiz in the draft section*

To assign the quiz

1. Select the quiz from the draft section in the **Assignment** tab.

2. Fill in any instructions, due dates, and who the assignment should
    be assigned to.

3. Click the **Assign** button to assign and save.

Note   If you do not want to assign the quiz at that moment, you can fill out the
quiz details and click **Save**, and the quiz will remain in a draft state until you
assign it at a later date.

Grades

As each assignment has been graded individually for each student, all of the grades are
compiled into a single tab named "Grades" at the top of your team. When you open the
tab, you will see a new column for each assignment that has been given during the class
as well as how well each student performed on that assignment. If you need to make any
adjustment to a grade, you can click the number, and once the cursor appears, type in
the adjusted number.

If you click the student name, you will navigate to their profile with a view of all
assignments that student turned in.

Tip You can give extra credit on assignment by giving additional points above the initial grading value. It will show as extra credit in the student's file.

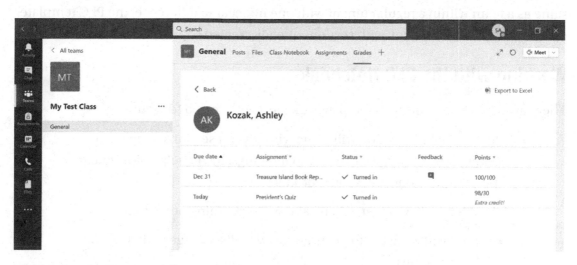

Figure 9-13. *Extra credit*

You can export any of your grade sheets to Excel by clicking the **Export to Excel** link in the upper-right corner of the screen. This can be useful if needing to provide a comprehensive list of the assignments and their details to parents or students.

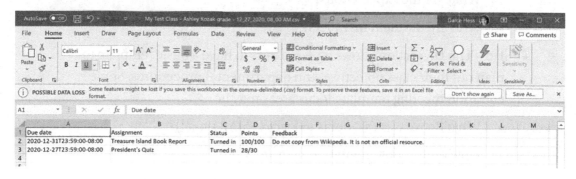

Figure 9-14. *Export to Excel*

Professional Learning Community

Professional Learning Community (PLC) templates are great for providing a working area specifically for teachers and administrators. This template works very much the same as a team within a regular tenant with one noticeable difference; the PLC template creates a OneNote Notebook with sections already created.

Working with the PLC Notebook

There are several sections with templates that are pre-created for you:

- Plan – The Plan section will come with several sections to help you manage your communication and meetings. It will help guide you to specific questions that should be answered:

  - When will we meet, where, and will everything be on time?

  - How will we listen to peers and how to discourage verbal interruptions?

  - What type of confidentiality is required?

  - How will the team arrive at decisions?

  - Is there an attendance policy?

  - What are the expectations?

  - Who are the team members?

- Do – The Do section allows for educators to have a basic template to plan out their class objectives and departmental procedures. Some common meeting template focus areas may be

  - What do we want students to learn (SMART goal)?

  - How is our implementation plan working?

  - What is the common assessment data telling us?

  - Are strategies working for students who have not attained proficiency?

  - Best practices.

  - Needs from the administration.

- Check – The Check section comes with a template to be able to analyze a student's progress based on the changes that have been implemented. It is a way to test to see if what you are doing as a teacher is working.

- Log – The Log section is placed to store links and information related to additional process narratives or external applications such as Sway that you might use to create presentations.

- Resources – The Resources section comes with a set of predefined training resources on how to use OneNote and the different sections in the team to be able to accomplish your goals.

Staff Template

The Staff template creates a team that is meant for communication, sharing important documents, and having a Staff Notebook to track common administrative goals. Like other teams, you can create separate channels, have conversations and meetings, and collaborate on documents.

Roles and Permissions

With a staff team, the staff leaders are the owners of the team. Anyone else that is added will be added as a member of the team. You can change who is an owner or a member of the team by clicking the **(...)** to the right of the team name and selecting **Manage Team**.

Staff Notebook

The Staff Notebook is a OneNote notebook that is automatically created when the team is created. Staff notebooks are great for keeping track of initiatives, meeting notes, links to additional resources, and action items. Like most notebooks, there are special permissions of what can and cannot be done by select groups of people. In Figure 9-15, we show the default section permissions for the notebook.

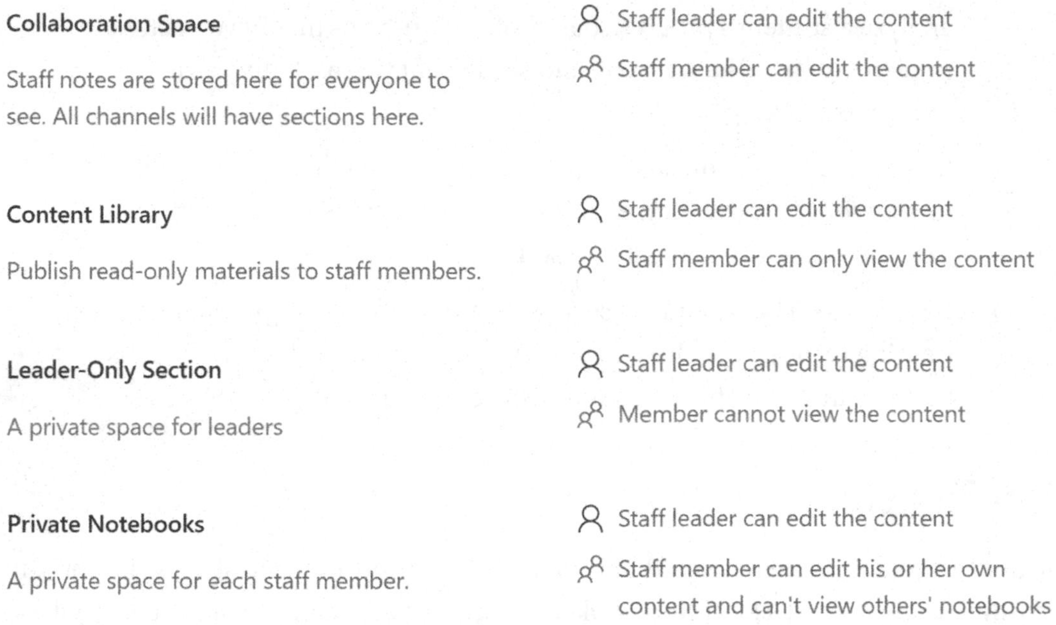

Collaboration Space

Staff notes are stored here for everyone to see. All channels will have sections here.

    ⚇ Staff leader can edit the content

    ⚇ Staff member can edit the content

Content Library

Publish read-only materials to staff members.

    ⚇ Staff leader can edit the content

    ⚇ Staff member can only view the content

Leader-Only Section

A private space for leaders

    ⚇ Staff leader can edit the content

    ⚇ Member cannot view the content

Private Notebooks

A private space for each staff member.

    ⚇ Staff leader can edit the content

    ⚇ Staff member can edit his or her own content and can't view others' notebooks

Figure 9-15. *Default settings for Staff Notebook*

Other Template

The Other template is a great template for student projects, extracurricular activities, sports teams, or clubs to have a place to communicate, share goals and documents, and interact. A student or a teacher has the ability to create these types of teams. This template does not come with a pre-made notebook, although you can add a tab and create a notebook, if needed.

Using Whiteboard During Meetings

Whiteboard is an app that can be used while in a Teams meeting. You can treat it just as if you were collaborating using a chalkboard or whiteboard within a classroom. This app works best if you have a touch screen or can use a digital pen to be able to write and draw out the concepts that you are trying to teach.

How to work with Whiteboard:

1. Start a Teams meeting.

2. Share your screen, and select **Whiteboard** from the screen options.

3. Select if you want only yourself to be able to edit or if you want everyone to be able to edit.

Whiteboard cannot be used on one-to-one meetings. It requires a minimum of three participants be in the meeting in order to be used.

Note   If you share a Whiteboard during a meeting, it will not be saved as part of the recording.

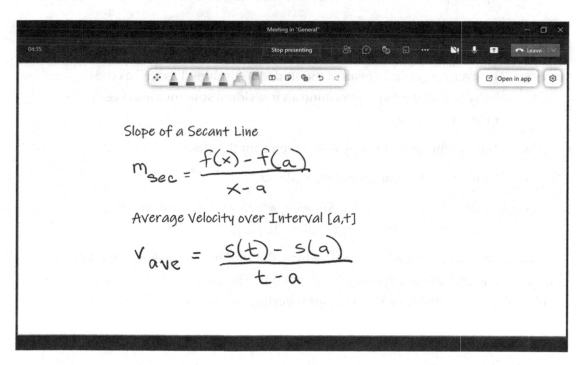

Figure 9-16. *Whiteboard*

Use Insights to Track Student Engagement

Insights is an app that is available to add as a tab in a team. It will allow you to track student engagement in your class and provide feedback and analytics. When teaching a remote class, it can be difficult to know if your students are paying attention, working on the assignment, or engaged in collaboration with other students. Then Insights app will help to give you instant feedback to help you with your student's engagement.

To add the Insights app

1. Click the + to add a new tab.

2. Search and select **Insights** app from the available apps.

3. The app will appear, but it will not produce any information until you create assignments, quizzes, and engage with students.

The Insights app will provide you with the following analytics:

- The percentage of Digital Activity of how many students are actively using Teams to complete their assignments and engaged

- The average grade from all of the students combined as well as the ability to drill down to determine an individual student's average grade on assignments.

- The percentage of on-time assignments for the class

- The average time for providing feedback

- Communication activity by knowing which students are creating, responding, and providing reactions to posts

You can hover and see what type of activity the student has been engaged in, from editing a document to participating in discussions. The analytics can also be exported to Excel to be viewed outside of Teams or for reporting purposes.

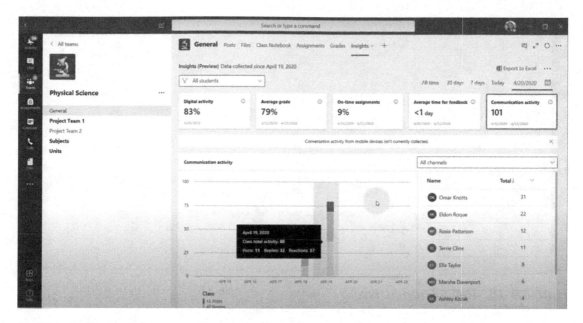

Figure 9-17. *Insights*

Gauge How Students Are Feeling with Reflect

Reflect is an app available from Microsoft to help gauge how students are feeling (SEL) in Microsoft Teams. In the world of remote learning, it can be challenging to understand how students are emotionally. The Reflect app offers an opportunity to connect with students in a private manner to see how they are doing.

The Reflect app offers several basic questions such as "How are you feeling today?". The question is then posted to the channel for students to click predefined smiley faces or provide additional information. The teacher should make sure that the private option is selected to ensure that the student's response and their name do not become public to other students. By selecting the private option, the students can respond, and the teacher will be the only person who can view the responses.

Note   A Systems Administrator must install the Reflect app in order for a teacher to add it to the team to use in a class.

Figure 9-18. *Reflect app in Teams*

Community and Training for Educators

Microsoft and the global community continue to provide many free and paid resources to help educators utilize Teams to create successful learning environments. Many courses are provided free of charge to help you get started.

Some resources to take note of are

- New Tools for Teaching Virtual Community
  `www.microsoft.com/en-us/store/workshops-training-and-events/educators`

- Request an in-person training for educators
  `https://customervoice.microsoft.com/Pages/ResponsePage.aspx?id=v4j5cvGGr0GRqy180BHbRxKuuH8O5eJLgsWdRZybuFZUODV XRExHRFA3MEs1V1JDVFpGUDIwSTBWUy4u`

Some of the ongoing classes that are offered:

- Back to school for the remote classroom – Teams for schools

- Microsoft Innovative Educator Training – Mobile Tools for Inclusive Classrooms

- Microsoft Teams Office Hours for Educators

- And many more…

Index

© Melissa Hubbard, Matthew J. Bailey, D'arce Hess, Mårten Hellebro 2021
M. Hubbard et al., *Mastering Microsoft Teams*, https://doi.org/10.1007/978-1-4842-6898-8

Printed in the United States
by Baker & Taylor Publisher Services